The Manual of Insight

(Vipassanā Dīpanī)

AND

The Noble Eightfold Path and its Factors Explained

(Maggaṅga-Dīpanī)

The Venerable Ledi Sayadaw

The Manual of Insight

Translated into English by

U Ñāṇa Mahāthera

AND

The Noble Eightfold Path and its Factors Explained

Translated into English by

U Saw Tun Teik

Revised edition by

Bhikkhu Khantipālo

BPS Pariyatti Editions

BPS Pariyatti Editions
An imprint of Pariyatti Publishing
www.pariyatti.org

Published by Buddhist Publication Society, Kandy, Sri Lanka, 1977, 1985, 1998.

Published with the consent of the original publisher. Copies of this book for sale in the Americas only.

First BPS Pariyatti Edition, 2017
ISBN: 978-1-938754-48-7 (Print)
ISBN: 978-1-938754-86-9 (PDF eBook)
ISBN: 978-1-938754-84-5 (ePub)
ISBN: 978-1-938754-85-2 (Mobi)
LCCN: 2013935066

Printed in the USA

Contents

The Manual of Insight

(Vipassanā Dīpanī)

The Noble Eightfold Path and Its Factors Explained

(Maggaṅga-dīpanī)

Publisher's Foreword to the American Edition

In recent years, many people in the West have been exposed to the teachings of the Buddha through the practice of Vipassana meditation as taught by S.N. Goenka. Mr. Goenka was born in Burma (now Myanmar) where he learned this technique of meditation from Sayagyi U Ba Khin, who had in turn been taught by Saya Thetgyi. Saya Thetgyi had the fortune to learn Vipassana from the highly respected scholar and meditator monk Ledi Sayadaw.

In Burma, Ledi Sayadaw is well known, and in his lifetime was the author of more than 100 books that provided both clarification and inspiration regarding the teachings of the Buddha. As Vipassana meditation in the tradition of Ledi Sayadaw begins to spread in the West, we are fortunate to begin to gain broader access to his writings as well.

We are grateful to the Buddhist Publication Society of Sri Lanka for allowing us to co-publish *The Manual of Insight* and *The Noble Eightfold Path and Its Factors Explained*. It is our sincere wish that this publication will prove valuable to those interested in understanding the Buddha's teaching at a deeper level, while providing the inspiration to continue walking step by step on the path.

The Manual of Insight

(Vipassanā Dīpanī)

THE MANUAL OF INSIGHT

(Vipassanā Dīpanī)

The Venerable Ledi Sayadaw

Translated into English by

U Ñāṇa Mahāthera

Vipassanā Dīpanī

The Exposition of Insight

The Three Hallucinations

Vipallāsa means hallucination, delusion, erroneous observation,[1] or taking that which is true as false and that which is false as true.

There are three kinds of hallucination:

1. *Saññā-vipallāsa*: hallucination of perception
2. *Citta-vipallāsa*: hallucination of thought
3. *Diṭṭhi-vipallāsa*: hallucination of views

Of those three, hallucination of perception is fourfold. It erroneously perceives:

- (i) Impermanence as permanence
- (ii) Impurity as purity
- (iii) Suffering as happiness
- (iv) No-soul as soul

The same holds good with regard to the remaining two hallucinations, those of thinking and views.

---

1 Another rendering, "illusion" may be proposed, which fits better for all three varieties, while "hallucination" strictly refers only to erroneous sense perception.—Editor.

All these classifications come under the category of "This is mine! This is my self or living soul!" and will be made clear later. The three hallucinations may be illustrated respectively by the similes of the wild deer, the magician, and a man who has lost his way.

The Simile of the Wild Deer

This is the simile of the wild deer to illustrate the hallucination of perception.

In the middle of a great forest a certain husbandman cultivated a piece of paddy land. While the cultivator was away, wild deer were in the habit of coming to the field and eating the young sprouts of growing grain. So the cultivator put some straw together into the shape of a man and set it up in the middle of the field in order to frighten the deer away. He tied the straw together with fibres into the semblance of a body, with head, hands, and legs; and with white lime painting on a pot the lineaments of a human face, he set it on the top of the body. He also covered the artificial man with some old clothes such as a coat, and so forth, and put a bow and arrow into his hands. Now the deer came as usual to eat the young paddy; but approaching it and catching sight of the artificial man, they took it for a real one, were frightened, and ran away.

In this illustration, the wild deer had seen men before and retained in their memory the perception of the shape and form of men. In accordance with their present perception, they took the straw man for a real man. Thus their perception was an erroneous perception. The hallucination of perception is as here shown in this allegory of the wild deer. It is very clear and easy to understand.

This particular hallucination is also illustrated by the case of a bewildered man who has lost his way and cannot make out the cardinal points, east and west, in the locality in which he is, although the rising and setting of the sun may be distinctly perceived by anyone with open eyes. If the error has once been made, it establishes itself very firmly, and can be removed only with great difficulty. There are many things within ourselves which we always apprehend erroneously and in a sense that is the reverse of the truth as regards impermanence and no-soul. Thus through the hallucination of perception we apprehend things erroneously in exactly the same way that the wild deer take the straw man to be a real man, even with their eyes wide open.

The Simile of the Magician

This is the simile of the magician to illustrate the hallucination of thought.

There is a sham art called magic by means of which, when lumps of earth are exhibited in the presence of a crowd, all who look at them think they are lumps of gold and silver. The power of the magical art takes from men their ordinary power of seeing and in its place puts an extraordinary kind of sight. It can thus for a time turn the mind upside down, so to speak. When persons are in command of themselves they see lumps of earth as they are. But under the influence of this magical art, they see the lumps of earth as lumps of gold and silver, with all their qualities of brightness, yellowness, whiteness, and so forth. Thus, their beliefs, observations, or ideas become erroneous. In the same way, our thoughts and ideas are in the habit of wrongly taking false things as true, and thus we delude ourselves. For instance, at night we are often deceived into thinking we see a man, when it is really the stump of a tree that we are looking at. Or, on seeing a bush, we imagine we are looking at a wild elephant; or, seeing a wild elephant, we take it to be a bush.

In this world all our mistaken ideas about things in our field of observation are due to the action of the hallucination of thought, which is deeper and more unfathomable than that of perception, since it deludes us by making false things seem true. However, as it is not so firmly rooted as the latter, it can easily be removed by investigation or by searching into the causes and conditions of things.

The Simile of the Man who has lost his Way

This is the simile of the man who has lost his way to illustrate the hallucination of views.

There was a large forest haunted by demons, who lived there, building towns and villages. Some travellers who were not acquainted with the roads came through the forest. The demons created their towns and villages as splendidly as those of the *devas*, or celestial beings, and assumed the forms of male and female devas. They also made the roads as pleasant and delightful as those of the devas. When the travellers saw these, they believed that these pleasant roads would lead them to large towns and villages, and so, turning aside from the right roads, they went astray following the wrong and misleading ones, arriving at the towns of the demons and suffering accordingly.

In this allegory, the large forest stands for the three worlds—of sense existence, fine-material, and immaterial existence. The travellers are all those who inhabit these worlds. The right road is right views; and the misleading road is wrong views. The right views here spoken of are of two kinds, namely, those that pertain to the world, and those pertaining to enlightenment. Of these two, the former connotes this right view: "All beings are the owners of their deeds; and every deed, both moral and immoral, committed by oneself, is one's own property and follows one throughout the whole long course of life," while the latter connotes the knowledge of the doctrine of causal genesis, of the aggregates, of the sense bases, and no-soul. Of these two views, the former is the right road to the round of existences. The worlds of the fortunate—the abodes of human beings, devas, and Brahmas—are like the towns of good people. The erroneous views that deny moral and immoral deeds and their results or effects are like the wrong, misleading roads. The worlds of the unfortunate—the abodes of the tortured, of animals, *petas*, and *asuras*—are like the towns of the demons.

The right view of knowledge, which is one of the factors of enlightenment, is like the right road that leads out of the round of existence. Nibbāna is like the town of good people.

The views "my body" and "my soul" are also like the wrong and misleading roads. Viewed in this light, the world comprising the abodes of human beings, devas, and Brahmas, or the ceaseless renewing of existences, is like the towns of the demons.

The aforesaid erroneous views belong likewise to the hallucinations, and are deeper and more firmly established than the hallucination of thought.

The Three Fantasies (*maññanā*)

Maññanā means fantasy, egotistic estimation, high imagination, or feigning to oneself that one is what one is not. Through ignorance, hallucination arises, and through hallucination fantasy arises.

Fantasy is of three kinds:

1. *Taṇhā-maññanā*: fantasy caused by craving
2. *Māna-maññanā*: fantasy caused by conceit
3. *Diṭṭhi-maññanā*: fantasy caused by wrong views

Of these, "fantasy caused by craving" means the high imagination: "This is mine! This is my own!" in clinging to what in reality is not "mine" and "my own." In strict truth, there is no "I" and as there is no "I," there can be no "mine" or "my own." Both personal and impersonal (external) objects are highly imagined and discriminated as, "This is mine; that other thing is not mine"; and "This is my own; that other thing is not mine." Such a state of imagination and fanciful discrimination is called "fantasy caused by craving."

"Personal objects" means one's own body and organs. "Impersonal (external) objects" means one's own relations, such as father, mother, and so forth, and one's own possessions.

"Fantasy caused by conceit" means high imagination of personal objects expressed as "I" or "I am." When it is supported or encouraged, so to speak, by personal attributes and impersonal objects, it becomes aggressively haughty and fantastically conceited.

Here personal attributes means vigour of eyes, ears, hands, legs, virtue, intuition, knowledge, possession of power, and so forth. Impersonal objects means plenitude of family, relations, surroundings, dwellings, possessions, and so forth.

"Fantasy caused by wrong views" means over-estimation of personal objects as "my bodily frame; my principle; my soul; the core, substance or essence of my being." In the expressions "earthen pots" and "earthen bowls," it is understood that earth is the substance of which these pots and bowls are made, and the very earth so made, so shaped, is again called pots and bowls. In the expressions "iron pots" and "iron bowls," and so forth, it is also understood that iron is the substance from which iron pots and bowls are made, and the very iron so made, so shaped, is again called pots and bowls. In exactly the same way that in these instances earth or iron is the substance from which the vessels are made, so the element of extension, the earth-element which pertains to the personality, is assumed to be the substance of living beings; and of the "I" this fanciful estimation of the facts of the case arises: "The element of extension is the living being: the element of extension is the 'I'." What is here said in connection with the element of extension is in like manner to be understood in connection with the element of cohesion, the liquid element, and all other elements found in a corporeal existence. This over-estimation or fantastic imagination will be expounded at greater length further on.

These three kinds of fantasy are also called the three *gāha*, or the three holds, to indicate their power of holding tightly and firmly. Since they also multiply erroneous, mistaken actions, which tend gradually but continuously to increase beyond all limits and never incline to cease, they are also called the three *papañcas* or the three multipliers.

The Two Dogmatic Beliefs (*abhinivesa*)

Abhinivesa means dogmatic belief, a strong belief set in the mind as firmly and immovably as doorposts, stone pillars, and monuments, so that it cannot be moved by any means or expenditure of effort. It is of two different kinds: (1) *taṇhābhinivesa*: dogmatic belief induced by craving; (2) *diṭṭhābhinivesa*: dogmatic belief induced by wrong views.

Of these, *taṇhābhinivesa* means the firm and unshakable belief in what is not "my own" body, head, hands, legs, eyes, nose, and so forth, as being "my own" body, head and so forth, throughout a long succession of existences, caused by attachment to the body.

Diṭṭhābhinivesa means the firm and unshakable belief in the existence of the soul or self or separate life in a person or creature, which is held, in accordance with this belief, to be an unchanging supreme thing that governs the body.

These two kinds of dogmatic belief are also called *taṇhā-nissaya* and *diṭṭhi-nissaya* respectively. They may also be called the two great reposers upon the five aggregates, and on body-and-mind; or the two great resting-places of *puthujjanas*, the ordinary men of the world.

The Two Stages (*bhūmi*)

Bhūmi (lit., soil, ground) means the stages where all creatures find their footing, generate, and grow. It is of two kinds: (1) *puthujjana-bhūmi*: the stage of the worldling; (2) *ariya-bhūmi*: the stage of the noble ones.

Puthujjana-bhūmi is the stage of the ordinary or normal being, the worldling (*puthujjana*); speaking in the sense of ultimate truth, it is nothing but the hallucination of views. All creatures of the ordinary worldly kind live in the world making this *diṭṭhi-vipallāsa*, or erroneous view, their resting place, their main support, their standing ground: "There is in me or in my body something that is permanent, pleasurable, and substantial."

The *diṭṭhi-maññanā* or fantasy through error, the *diṭṭhi-gāha* or erroneous hold, the *diṭṭhi-papañca* or multiplier of error, and the *diṭṭhi-abhinivesa* or strong belief induced by error, are also the landing stages, the supports, the resting places, and the standing grounds of all *puthujjanas*. Hence they will never be released from the state or existence of a puthujjana, so long as they take their firm stand on the ground of the aforesaid many-named error.

As to the *ariya-bhūmi*, it is a state of an *ariya*, a noble and sanctified being, in whom hallucination is eradicated. It is, speaking in the ultimate sense, nothing but this right view, this right apprehension, the right understanding: "There is in me or in my body nothing permanent, pleasurable, and substantial." As an ariya lives making right view his main footing, this right view may be called the stage of the ariya. Upon the attainment of this right view, a being is said to have transcended the *puthujjana-bhūmi*, and to have set foot on the *ariya-bhūmi*.

Among the innumerable ordinary beings who have been treading the ground of the state of being puthujjana during countless existences of unknown beginning, if a certain person trying to eradicate the hallucination of error and to implant right view within himself, on a certain day succeeds in his attempts, he is said to have set foot that self-same day upon the ground of the ariya and to have become an ariya, that is, a sanctified being. Even if there should remain the hallucinations of thought and perception in some of the ariyas, they would not commit such evil deeds as would produce for them evil effects in the worlds of misfortune, for they have eradicated the weighty hallucination of error. The two remaining hallucinations would merely enable them to enjoy such worldly pleasures as they have lawfully earned.

The Two Destinations (*gati*)

Gati means literally "going," that is, going from life to life by way of rebirth; in other words, the change of existences, or the future destination of beings. It is of two kinds: (1) *puthujjana-gati*: the destination of worldlings; (2) *ariya-gati*: the destination of sanctified beings.

The former signifies the taking rebirth of the ordinary person, the worldling, which is dispersive (*vinipātana*). That is to say, he cannot be reborn into whatever kind of existence he might wish, but is liable to fall into any of the thirty-one kinds of existence, according as he is thrown by his past kamma. Just as, when a coconut, or any other fruit, falls from a tree, it cannot be ascertained beforehand where it will come to rest; so also when a worldling is reborn after his death, it cannot be known beforehand where he will be reborn. Every creature that comes into life inevitably has to face the evil of death; and after his death he is also sure to fall by dispersion into any type of existence. Thus the two great evils of death and dispersion are inseparably linked to every being born.

Of these two, the dispersion of life after death is worse than death; for the four realms of misery down to the Avīci hell stand wide open to a worldling who departs from the world of men; they are open to him like unobstructed space. As soon as his term of life ends, he may fall into any of the realms of woe. Whether far or near, there is no intervening period of time between two existences. In the wink of an eyelid, he may be reborn as an animal, as a wretched ghost (*peta*), as a titan or asūra, an enemy of Sakka, the king of gods. The same possibility holds if he dies in any of the six upper realms of the sphere of sense existence (*kāmāvacara-deva*). But when he expires from the fine-material (*rūpa-loka*), or immaterial worlds (*arūpa-loka*), there is no direct fall into the four realms of misery; there is a halt of one existence either in the abode of men or in those of devas, wherefrom he may fall into those four worlds of misery.

Why do we say that every being fears death? Because death is followed by dispersion to any sphere of existence. If there were no dispersion as regards existence after death, and one could take rebirth in any existence at one's choice, no one would fear death so much, although, to be sure, sometimes there may be thirst for death when a being, after living a considerable length of time in one existence, desires to move to a new one.

By way of showing how great is the dispersion of existence in the case of a worldling, the similes of the fingernail (Nakhasikha Sutta) and of the blind turtle (Kāṇakacchapa Sutta) may be cited from the discourses.

Nakhasikha Sutta (The Sutta on the Fingernail)

At one time the Buddha, showing them some dust which he had taken upon the tip of his fingernail, addressed the disciples thus:

> "If, O bhikkhus, these few grains of dust upon my fingernail and all the dust of the universe were com-

pared in quantity, which would you say was less, and which more?" The disciples replied: "Lord, the dust on your fingernail is less, and that of the universe is more. Surely, Lord, the dust on your fingernail is not worthy of mention in comparison with the dust of the universe." Then the Buddha continued: "Even so, bhikkhus, those who are reborn in the abodes of men and devas when they have expired, are very few even as the few grains of dust on my fingernail; and those who are reborn in the four realms of misery are exceedingly many, even as the dust of the great universe. Again, those who have expired from the four miserable worlds and are reborn in the abodes of men and devas are few even as the grains of dust on my fingernail; and those who are repeatedly reborn in the four miserable worlds are innumerable, even as the grains of dust of the great universe."

What has just been said is the substance of the Nakhasikha Sutta. But, to say nothing of the beings of all the four realms of misery, the creatures that inhabit the four great oceans alone will suffice to make evident how great is the evil of dispersion (*vinipātana-gati*), the variety of possible kinds of existence after death.

Kāṇakacchapa Sutta (The Sutta on the Blind Turtle)

At one time the Buddha addressed the disciples thus:

"There is, O bhikkhus, in the ocean a blind turtle. He plunges into the water of the unfathomable ocean and swims about incessantly in any direction wherever his head may lead. There is also in the ocean

> the yoke of a cart which is ceaselessly floating about on the surface of the water, and is carried away in all directions by tide, current, and wind. Thus these two go on throughout an incalculable space of time. Perchance it happens that in the course of time the yoke arrives at the precise place and time where and when the turtle puts up his head, and yokes on to it. Now, O bhikkhus, is it possible that such a time might come as is said?" "In ordinary truth, Lord," replied the bhikkhus, "it is impossible; but time being so vast, and an aeon lasting so long, it may be admitted that perhaps at some time or other it might be possible for the two to yoke together, as said: if the blind tortoise lives long enough, and the yoke does not rot and break up before such a coincidence comes to pass."

Then the Buddha said:

> "Bhikkhus, the occurrence of such a strange thing is not to be counted a difficult one; for there is a still greater, a harder, a hundred times, a thousand times more difficult thing than this lying hidden from your knowledge. And what is this? It is, bhikkhus, the obtaining of a human existence again by a man who has expired and been reborn once in any of the four realms of misery. The occurrence of the yoking of the blind tortoise is not worth thinking of as a difficult occurrence in comparison therewith. Because only those who perform good deeds and abstain from bad actions can obtain the existence of men and devas. The beings in the four miserable worlds cannot discern what is virtuous and what vicious, what good and what bad, what moral and

> what immoral, what meritorious and what demeritorious; consequently, they live a life of immorality and demerit, tormenting one another with all their power. Those creatures of the hells and the ghost world in particular live a very miserable life on account of punishments and torments which they experience with sorrow, pain and distress. Therefore, O bhikkhus, the opportunity of being reborn in the abode of men is a hundred times, a thousand times harder to obtain than the encountering of the blind turtle with the yoke."

According to this sutta, why those creatures who are born in the miserable planes are far from human existence is because they never look up but always look down. And what is meant by looking down? The ignorance in them by degrees becomes greater and stronger from one existence to another; and as the water of a river always flows down to the lower plains, so also they are always tending towards the lower existences; for the ways towards the higher existences are closed to them, while those towards the lower existences are freely open. This is the meaning of "looking down." Hence, from this story of the blind turtle, the wise apprehend how great, how fearful, how terribly perilous are the evils of the worldling's destination, i.e., the "dispersion of existence."

What has been said concerns the *puthujjana-gati*. Now, what is the *ariya-gati*, the destination of sanctified beings? It is deliverance from the dispersion of existence after death. It is also the potentiality of being reborn in higher existences or in existences according to one's choice. It is not like the fall of coconuts from trees, but is to be compared to birds which fly through the air to whatsoever place or tree they may wish to perch on. Those men, devas, and Brahmas who have attained the ariya state, can go to whatever better existence—as men, devas, Brahmas—they may wish to be reborn into, when they expire from the particular existence in which they have attained such ariya state. Though they expire unexpectedly without aiming to be reborn in a particular existence, they are destined to be reborn in a better or higher existence, and at the same time are entirely free from rebirth into lower and miserable existences. Moreover, if they are reborn again in the abode of men, they never become of the lower or poorer classes, nor are they fools or heretics, but become quite otherwise. It is the same in the abodes of devas and Brahmas. They are entirely set free from the *puthujjana-gati*.

What has been said concerns the destination of ariyas.

Explanation of the Two Destinations

Now we will explain the two destinations side by side.

When a man falls from a tree, he falls like a coconut because he has no wings with which to fly in the air. In precisely the same way, when men, devas, and Brahmas who are worldlings riveted to the hallucination of wrong views and not having the wings of the Noble Eightfold Path to make the sky their resting-place, are reborn after the dissolution of their present bodies into new ones. They fall tumbling into the bonds of the evils of dispersion. In this world ordinary men who climb up very high trees fall tumbling to the ground when the branches which they clutch, or try to make their resting-place, break. They suffer much pain from the fall, and sometimes death ensues because they have no other resting-places but the branches, neither have they wings to fly in the air. It is the same with men, devas, and Brahmas who have the hallucination of wrong views: when their resting-place of wrong views as regards self breaks down, they fall tumbling into the dispersion of existence. For their resting-places are only their bodies; and they have neither such a resting-place as Nibbāna nor strong wings like the Noble Eightfold Path to support them.

As for the birds, though the branches they rest on may break, they never fall, but easily fly through the air to any other tree. For the branches are not their permanent resting-places but only temporary ones. They entirely rely on their wings and the air. In the same way, men, devas, and Brahmas who have become ariyas and are freed from the hallucination of wrong views, neither regard their bodies as their self, nor rely upon them. They have in their possession permanent resting-places, such as Nibbāna, which is the entire cessation of all tumbling existences. They also possess the very mighty wings of the Noble Eightfold Path which are able to bear them to better existences.

The Two Truths (*sacca*)

Sacca or truth is the constant faithfulness or concordance of the term which names a thing, to or with that thing's intrinsic nature. It is of two kinds: 1. *sammuti-sacca*: conventional or relative truth; 2. *paramattha-sacca*: or ultimate truth.

Of the two, conventional truth is the truthfulness of the customary terms used by the great majority of people, such as "self exists," "men exist," "devas exist," "Sakkas exist," "elephants exist," "my head exists," and so on. This conventional truth is the opposite of untruth, and so on can overcome it. It is not a lie or lack of truthfulness when people say: "There probably exists an immutable, permanent, and continuing self or living soul which is neither momentarily rising nor passing away throughout one existence," for this is the customary manner of speech of the great majority of people who have no intention whatever of deceiving others. But according to ultimate truth, it is reckoned a *vipallāsa* or hallucination, which erroneously regards the impermanent as permanent and non-self as self. So long as this erroneous view remains undestroyed, one can never escape from the evils of *saṃsāra*, the wheel of life. All this holds good when people say "a person exists," and so on.

Ultimate truth is the absolute truthfulness of assertion or negation in full and complete accordance with what is actual: the elementary, fundamental qualities of phenomena. Here stating such truth in affirmative form, one may say: "The element of solidity exists," "the element of extension exists," "the element of cohesion exists," "the element of kinetic energy exists," "mind exists," "consciousness exists," "contact, feeling, and perception exist," "material aggregates exist," and so on. And expressing such truth in a negative form, it can be said: "No self exists," "no living soul exists," "no person exists," "no being exists," "nor do hands, nor any members of the body exist," "neither does a man exist nor a deva," and so on. In saying here: "No self exists," "no living soul exists," we mean that there is no such ultimate entity as a self or living soul which persists unchanged during the whole term of life, without momentarily coming to be and passing away. In the expressions "No being exists," and so forth, what is meant is that nothing actually exists but material and mental elements. These elements are neither persons nor beings, nor men, nor devas, etc. Therefore there is no separate being or person apart from the elements. This ultimate truth is the diametrical opposite of the hallucination, and so can confute it. One who is thus able to confute or reject the hallucination can escape from the evils of *saṃsāra*.

According to conventional truth, a person exists, a being exists; a person or a being continually transmigrates from one existence to another in the ocean of life. But according to ultimate truth, neither a person nor a being exists and there is no one who transmigrates from one existence to another. Here it may be asked: "Do not these two truths seem to be as poles asunder?" Of course they seem to be so. Nevertheless, we may bring them together. Have we not said: "according to conventional truth" and "according to ultimate truth"? Each kind of truth accordingly is truthful as regards its own mode of expression. Hence, if one man should say that there exists a person or a being according to conventional truth, the other to whom he speaks ought not to contradict him, for these conventional terms describe what apparently exists. And likewise, if the other says that there exists neither a person nor a being according to ultimate truth, the former ought not to deny this, for, in the ultimate sense, material and mental phenomena alone truly exist, and in strict reality they know no person or being.

For example: men dig up lumps of earth from certain places, pound them into dust, knead this dust with water into clay, and from this clay make various kinds of useful pots, jars, and cups. Thus there exist various kinds of pots, jars and cups in the world.

Now, when discussion takes place on this subject, if it were asked: "Are there earthen pots and cups in this world?" the answer according to the conventional truth should be given in the affirmative, and according to the ultimate truth in the negative, since this kind of truth admits only the positive existence of the earth out of which the pots and so forth were made. Of these two answers the former requires no explanation inasmuch as it is an answer according to the established usage, but as regards the latter, some explanation is needed. In the objects that we called "earthen pots," and "earthen cups," what really exists is only earth not pots or cups in the sense of ultimate truth, for the term "earth" applies properly not to pots and cups but to actual substantial earth. There are also pots and cups made of iron, brass, silver, and gold. These cannot be called earthen pots and cups, since they are not made of earth. The terms "pots" and "cups" also are not terms descriptive of earth but of ideas derived from the appearance of pots and cups, such as their circular or spherical shape and so on. This is obvious, because the terms "pots" and "cups" are not applied to the mere lumps of earth which have no shape or form of pots and cups. Hence it follows that the term "earth" is not a term descriptive of pots and cups, but of real earth; and also the terms "pots" and "cups" are not terms descriptive of earth but of pictorial ideas (*saṇṭhāna-paññatti*) which have no elementary substance other than the dust of clay, being mere conceptions presented to the mind by the particular appearance, form, and shape of the worked-up clay. Hence the negative statement according to the ultimate truth, namely, that "no earthen pots and cups exist," ought to be accepted without question.

Material Phenomena

Now we come to the analysis of things in the ultimate sense. Of the two kinds of ultimate phenomena, material and mental, as mentioned above, the former is of twenty-eight kinds:

(i) The four great essential elements:

1. Element of solidity (*paṭhavī*)
2. Element of cohesion, or binding, the fluid (*āpo*)
3. Element of heat, including warmth and cold (*tejo*)
4. Element of motion or vibration (*vāyo*)

(ii) The six bases:

5. Eye-base
6. Ear-base
7. Nose-base
8. Tongue-base
9. Body-base
10. Heart-base

(iii) The two sexes:

11. Male sex
12. Female sex

(iv) One species of physical life:

13. Vital force

(v) One species of material nutrition:

14. Edible food

(vi) The four sense fields:

15. Visible form
16. Sound
17. Odour
18. Savour

These last eighteen species are called genetic material qualities (*jāta-rūpāni*), as they possess the power of production.

(vii) One species of physical limitation:

19. Element of space

(viii) The two communications:

20. Intimation through the body
21. Intimation through speech

(ix) The three plasticities:

22. Lightness
23. Pliancy
24. Adaptability

(x) The four salient features:

25. Integration
26. Continuance
27. Decay
28. Impermanence or death

These last ten species are called non-genetic material qualities (*ajāta-rūpāni*) as they do not possess the power of production.

Four Great Essentials (*mahābhūta*)

Mahābhūta means to develop greatly.

1. The element of extension is the element of earth, that is, the fundamental principle or foundation of matter. It exists in gradations of many kinds, such as hardness, more hardness, stiffness, more stiffness, softness, more softness, pliability, more pliability, and so on.

2. The element of cohesion is the element of water, that is, the cohesive power of material qualities whereby

they form into a mass or bulk or a lump. There are apparently many kinds of cohesion.

3. The element of heat is the element of fire, that is, the power to burn, to inflame, and to mature the material qualities. This maturative quality is of two kinds, namely, the maturative quality of heat and the maturative quality of cold.

4. The element of motion is the element of wind or air, that is, the power of supporting or resisting. It is of many kinds, such as supportive, resistive, conveying, vibratory, diffusive, and so on.

From these four great elements all other forms of matter are born. Or, expressed in another way: All matter is a combination, in one proportion or another, of these four elementary properties, together with a varying number of secondary material phenomena derived from the great elements.

Derived Materiality (upādā-rūpa)

The Six Bases (*vatthu*)

A base, *vatthu*, is that where consciousness is generated, arises, develops, or that whereupon it depends.

5. The eye-base is the sensorium within the eyeball where consciousness of sight is generated: consciousness of sight connotes the power of seeing various kinds of colours, appearances, forms and shapes.

6. The ear-base is the sensorium within the organ of the ear where consciousness of sound is generated; and the consciousness of sound connotes the power of hearing various kinds of sound.

7. The nose-base is the sensorium within the nose organ where consciousness of smell is generated; and the consciousness of smell connotes the power of smelling different kinds of odours.

8. The tongue-base is the sensorium upon the surface of the tongue where consciousness of taste is generated; the consciousness of taste connotes the power of tasting many kinds of taste such as sweet, sour, and so forth.

9. The body-base is the sensorium locating itself by pervading the whole body within and without from head to foot, where consciousness of touch is generated; the consciousness of touch connotes the power of feeling or sensing physical contacts.

10. The heart-base (*hadaya-vatthu*) is a kind of very fine, bright, subtle matter within the organ of heart where mind consciousness, comprising sixty-nine classes of the same in number is generated.

From these six bases all classes of consciousness are generated and arise.

The Two Sexes (*bhāva*)

Bhāva means production or productive principle.

11. The *itthi-bhāva,* the female sex, is a certain productive principle of matter which produces several different kinds of female features or feminine characteristics.

12. The *puṃ-bhāva,* the male sex, is a certain productive principle of matter which produces several different kinds of male features or appearances and masculine characteristics.

The two sexes respectively locate themselves in the bodies of male and female, like the body-base they pervade the entire frame from the sole of the foot to the top of the head within and without. Owing to their predominant features the distinction between femininity and masculinity and femininity is readily discerned.

The Vital Force (*jīvita-rūpa*)

13. *Jīvita* means life, that is, the vital force which controls the material qualities produced by kamma, and keeps them fresh in the same way that the water of a pond preserves the lotus plants from decay. It so informs them as to prevent them from withering. The common expressions of ordinary speech, "a being lives" or "a being dies," are descriptive merely of the presence or absence of this material quality of life. When it ceases forever with reference to a particular form, we say "a

being dies," and we say "a being lives" so long as it continues to act in any particular form. This also permeates the whole body.

Material Nutrition (*āhāra-rūpa*)

14. *Āhāra-rūpa* means the element of essential nutriment that nourishes or promotes the growth of material qualities. Just as the element of water that resides in earth or falls from the sky nourishes trees or plants, or mainly promotes their growth and helps them to fecundate, develop and last long, so also this material quality of nutrition nourishes the four kinds of matter produced by the four causes kamma, mind, temperature, and food,—and helps them to fecundate and grow. It is the main supporter of the material quality of life, so that undertaking various kinds of work in the world for the sake of getting one's daily food is called a man's living or livelihood.

The Four Sense Fields (*gocara-rūpa*)

Gocara means sense field or object of the five senses.

15. The object "visible form" is the quality of colour and shape of various objects.

16. The object "sound" is the quality of sound itself.

17. The object "odour" is the quality of scent or smell.

18. The object "savour" is the quality of savour or taste.

Mention is not made here of touch, the tangible object, as it consists of three of the great elements, namely, tangible extension, tangible temperature, and tangible movement. Counting the tangible also, we thus get five sense fields in all. Of these, visible form is the object of eye; sound, of ear; odour, of nose; savour, of tongue; and the tangible, of body.

The Element of Space (*ākāsa-dhātu*)

19. *Ākāsa-dhātu* means the element of space. In a heap of sand there is space between each particle of sand. Hence we may say that there are as many spaces as there are particles of sand in the heap; and we can also distinguish the particles of sand from one another. When the heap is destroyed, the particles of sand are scattered about, and the space enclosed between them disappears also. Similarly, in very hard lumps of stone, marble, iron, and other metals, there are innumerable atoms and particles of atoms, called *kalāpas* or groups. Even the finest, smallest particles of an atom contain at least the following eight qualities of matter: the four essentials and colour, odour, savour, and nutritive essence. And each group is separated by the element of space located between them. Therefore there is at least as much space as there is matter in the lump. It is owing to the existence of this space that lumps of stone and iron can be broken up, or cut into pieces, or pounded into dust, or melted.

The Two Modes of Communications (*viññatti-rūpa*)

Viññatti-rūpa means mode of communication. It is a sign employed to communicate the willingness, intention, or purpose, of one person to the understanding of another.

20. *Kāya-viññatti* is that peculiar movement of body by which one's purpose is made known to others.

21. *Vacī-viññatti* is that peculiar movement of sounds in speech by which one's purpose is made known to others.

Those who cannot see the minds of others know the purpose, the intention, the willingness of others through the use of these two modes of communication. These two are employed not only in communicating one's purpose or intention to the understanding of another, but also in moving the parts of the body while walking, and so forth, according to one's will, as also in learning by heart, reading to one-self, and so forth.

The Three Plasticities (*vikāra-rūpa*)

Vikāra means the peculiar expression or distinctive condition of the genetic material qualities (*jāta-rūpa*).

22. *Lahutā* is the lightness of the material quality.

23. *Mudutā* is the pliancy of the material qualities.

24. *Kammaññatā* is the adaptability of the two media of communication.

When one of the Four Great Essentials falls out of order and becomes disproportionate to the rest in any parts of the body, these parts are not light as usual in applying themselves to some work, but tend to become heavy and awkward; they are not pliable as usual, but tend to become hard, coarse, and rigid; they are not as adaptable as usual in their movements in accord with one's will, but tend to become difficult and strained. Likewise, when the essentials are out of order the tongue and the lips, are not adaptable according to one's wish in speaking, but become firm and stiff. When the four great essentials are in good order and the parts of the body are in sound health, the matter of the body (*rūpa*) is said to be in possession of these qualities, lightness, pliancy, and adaptability, which are called the three plasticities (*vikāra-rūpa*).

The Four Salient Features (*lakkhaṇa-rūpa*)

Lakkhaṇa means the salient feature or mark by means of which it is decisively known that all material and mental qualities are subject to impermanence.

25. *Upacaya-rūpa* means both integration and continuance of integration; the former may be called *ācaya* (initial integration) and the latter *upacaya* (sequential integration).

26. *Santati-rūpa* means continuance. From the cessation of sequential integration to the commencement of decay the phenomenon continues without any increase or decrease. And such a continuous state of material phenomenon is called *santati* or *pavatti* (prolongation). The production (*jāti*) of the groups of material qualities alone is described by the three names, *ācaya*, *upacaya*, and *santati*.

27. *Jaratā* is the state of growing old, of decline, of maturity, ripeness (in the sense of being ready to fall), decay, caducity, rottenness, or corruption.

28. *Aniccatā* means impermanence, death, termination, cessation, brokenness or the state of disappearing.[2]

---

2 It is our Ledi Sayādaw's style in writing to express an idea by means of as many synonymous terms as he can collect. A translator such as I, who has not fully attained the mastery of the English language, in which the treasures of Burmese literature are to be

A plant has five periods, the *ācaya* period, the *upacaya* period, the *santati* period, the *jaratā* period, and the *aniccatā* period. It is first generated; then it grows up gradually or develops day-by-day; and after the cessation of growth it stands for sometime in the fully developed state. After that it begins to decay, and at last it dies and disappears.

Here, the primary generation of the material qualities is called *ācaya* period; the gradual growth or development, the *upacaya* period; and their fully developed state, the *santati* period. However, during these three periods there are momentary decays (*khaṇika-jaratā*) and momentary deaths (*khaṇika-aniccatā*), but they are inconspicuous. The declining of the plant is called *jaratā* period. During the period of decline there are momentary births (*khaṇika-jāti*) and momentary deaths (*khaṇika-maraṇa*), but they are also inconspicuous.[3] The death of the plant and the final disappearance of all its constituents are called the *aniccatā* period. During what we call death there are also momentary births and decays but they are invisible. The five periods allotted to what is apparent to the view are shown here only in order to help one to grasp the idea of *lakkhaṇa-rūpas*.

In a similar manner we may divide, in the life of a fruit tree, the branches, the leaves, the buds, the flowers, and the fruits into five periods each. A fruit can be divid-

---

deposited, meets difficulty with furnishing the translation with a sufficient number of appropriate terms.—Translator

3 The commentator of the Dhammasaṅgaṇī, in his *Atthasālinī*, explains this by an illustration of a well dug out on the bank of a river. The first gushing out of water in the well, he says, is like the ācaya of the material phenomenon; the flushing up or the gradual increasing or the rising up of water to the full, is like the *upacaya*; and the flooding is like the *santati*.—Tr.

ed into five periods thus: the first period of appearance; the second period of growth or development; the third period of standing; the fourth period of ripening and decaying; and the fifth period of falling from the stem, total destruction, or final disappearance.

Just as we get five periods in the life of plants, so is it with all creatures, and also with all their bodily parts; with their movements or bodily actions such as going, coming, standing, and sitting; with their speech and with their thought. The beginning, the middle, and the end are all to be found in the existence of every material thing.

The Four Producers of Material Phenomena

There are four producers (*samuṭṭhāna*) which produce material phenomena: (1) *kamma*, (2) *citta*, (3) *utu*, (4) *āhāra*.

1. *Kamma* means moral and immoral actions committed in previous existences.
2. *Citta* means mind and mental concomitants existing in the present life.
3. *Utu* means the two states of *tejo-dhātu*, the fire-element; heat (*uṇha-tejo*) and cold (*sīta-tejo*).
4. *Āhara* means the two kinds of nutritive essence: internal nutriment that obtains from the time of conception, and external nutriment that exists in edible food.

Out of the twenty-eight species of material qualities, nine species—the six bases, two sexes, and life are produced only by kamma. The two media of communications are produced only by *citta*.

Sound is produced by *citta* and *utu*. The three plasticities are produced by *citta, utu*, and *āhāra*. Of the remaining thirteen, excluding *jaratā* (decay) and *aniccatā* (impermanence), the eleven—comprising the four great essentials, nutriment, visible form, odour, savour, the element of space, integration, and continuance—are produced by the four causes. These eleven always appertain severally to the four classes of phenomena produced by the four causes. There are no phenomena that enter into composition without these. Material phenomena enter into composition with these, forming groups of eight, nine, and so forth, and each group is called *rūpa-kalāpa*.

Two salient features, decay and impermanence, are excluded from the material qualities born of the four causes as they disorganise what has been produced.

Mental Phenomena

There are fifty-four kinds of mental phenomena: *citta*: mind or consciousness; *cetasika*: mental properties or concomitants, fifty-two in number; and *nibbāna*: liberation from the circle of existences.[4]

Citta means the faculty of investigating an object (*ārammaṇa*); or of taking possession of an object; or of knowing an object; or of being conscious of an object. *Cetasikas* are factors of consciousness, or mental properties born of mind, or concomitants of mind. *Nibbāna* means freedom from all suffering.

---

4 Nibbāna is here regarded as a mental phenomenon, not from the objective, but from the subjective point of view.—Tr.

Consciousness

Consciousness is divided into six classes:

1. Consciousness of sight
2. Consciousness of sound
3. Consciousness of smell
4. Consciousness of taste
5. Consciousness of touch
6. Consciousness of mind

Of these:

1. The consciousness arising at the eye-base is called consciousness of sight, and has the function of seeing.

2. The consciousness arising at the ear-base is called consciousness of sound, and has the function of hearing.

3. The consciousness arising at the nose-base is called consciousness of smell, and has the function of smelling.

4. The consciousness arising at the tongue-base is called consciousness of taste, and has the function of tasting.

5. The consciousness arising at the body-base is called consciousness of touch, and has the function of touching.

6. The consciousness arising at the heart-base is called consciousness of mind. In the immaterial world (*arūpa-loka*), however, mind-consciousness arises without any physical base.

Mind-consciousness is again subdivided into four kinds:

(a) *Kāma*-consciousness
(b) *Rūpa*-consciousness
(c) *Arūpa*-consciousness
(d) *Lokuttara*-consciousness

Of these:

(a) *Kāma*-consciousness is that which is under the dominance of desire prevailing in the world of sense desire (*kāma-loka*). It is fourfold, thus: moral (*kusala*) immoral (*akusala*), resultant (*vipāka*), and ineffective (i.e., kammically inoperative, *kriyā*).

(b) *Rūpa*-consciousness is the *jhānic* mind which has become free from sense-desire but still remains under the dominance of the desire prevailing in the fine-material world. It is threefold, thus: moral, resultant, and ineffective.

(c) *Arūpa*-consciousness is also the *jhānic* mind which has become free from desire for the fine-material, but still remains under the dominance prevailing in the immaterial world. It is also threefold, thus: moral, resultant, and ineffective.

(d) *Lokuttara*, or supramundane consciousness, is the noble mind (*ariya-citta*) which has become free from the threefold desire, and has transcended the three planes, *kāma*, *rūpa*, and *arūpa*. It is of two kinds, thus: noble consciousness in the path (of stream-entry, etc.) and noble consciousness in the fruition (of stream-entry, etc.).

Cetasikas or Mental Properties

Mental properties are of fifty-two kinds.

(a) The seven common properties (*sabba-citta-sādhāraṇa*), so called on account of being common to all classes of consciousness:

1. *Phassa*: contact
2. *Vedanā*: feeling
3. *Saññā*: perception
4. *Cetanā*: volition
5. *Ekaggatā*: concentration of mind
6. *Jīvita*: psychic life
7. *Manasikāra*: attention

(b) The six particulars (*pakiṇṇaka*), so called because they are features only of certain types of consciousness:

8. *Vitakka*: initial application
9. *Vicāra*: sustained application
10. *Viriya*: effort
11. *Pīti*: pleasurable interest
12. *Chanda*: desire-to-do
13. *Adhimokkha*: decision

The above thirteen mental properties are called "mixers"[5] (*vomissaka*), meaning that they can mix with both moral and immoral consciousness. Shwe Zan Aung calls them "un-moral properties."

5 *Vomissaka* literally means "mixed" or "miscellaneous".—Ed.

(c) The fourteen immoral properties (*akusala*) are:

14. *Lobha*: greed
15. *Dosa*: hate
16. *Moha*: dullness
17. *Diṭṭhi*: error
18. *Māna*: conceit
19. *Issā*: envy
20. *Macchariya*: selfishness
21. *Kukkucca*: worry
22. *Ahirika*: shamelessness
23. *Anottappa*: recklessness
24. *Uddhacca*: distraction
25. *Thīna*: sloth
26. *Viddha*: torpor
27. *Vicikicchā*: perplexity

(d) The twenty-five moral properties (*sobhana*) are:

28. *Alobha*: disinterestedness; lit.: non-greed
29. *Adosa*: amity; lit.: non-hate
30. *Amoha*: reason; lit.: non-delusion
31. *Saddhā*: faith
32. *Sati*: mindfulness
33. *Hiri*: modesty
34. *Ottappa*: discretion
35. *Tatramajjhattatā*: balance of mind
36. *Kāyapassaddhi*: composure of mental properties
37. *Cittapassaddhi*: composure of mind
38. *Kāyalahutā*: buoyancy of mental properties
39. *Cittalahutā*: buoyancy of mind
40. *Kāyamudutā*: pliancy of mental properties
41. *Cittamudutā*: pliancy of mind
42. *Kāyakammaññatā*: adaptability of mental properties

43. *Cittakammaññatā*: adaptability of mind
44. *Kāyapaguññatā*: proficiency of mental properties
45. *Cittapaguññatā*: proficiency of mind
46. *Kāyujukatā*: rectitude of mental properties
47. *Cittujukatā*: rectitude of mind
48. *Sammā-vācā*: right speech
49. *Sammā-kammantā*: right action
50. *Sammā-ājīva*: right livelihood
51. *karuṇā*: pity
52. *muditā*: appreciation.

The Common Properties

1. *Phassa* means contact, and contact means the faculty of pressing the object so as to cause the agreeable or disagreeable "sap" to come out. So contact is the main principle or prime mover of the mental properties in their uprising. If the sap cannot be squeezed out, then no object will be of any use.

2. *Vedanā* means feeling, the faculty of tasting the sapid flavour thus squeezed out by *phassa*. All creatures are sunk in feeling.

3. *Saññā* means perception, the act of perceiving. All creatures become wise through this perception, if they perceive things with sufficient clarity in accordance with their own ways, customs, creeds, and so forth.

4. *Cetanā* means volition, the faculty of determining the activities of the mental concomitants so as to bring them into harmony. In the common speech of the world we are accustomed to say of one who supervises a piece of work that he is the performer or author of the work. We usually say: "Oh, this work was done by So-and-so" or "This is such and such a person's great

work." It is somewhat the same in connection with the ethical aspects of things. Volition is called action (*kamma*), as it determines the activities of the mental concomitants and supervises all the actions of body, speech, and mind. As all prosperity in this life is the outcome of the exertions put forth in work performed with body, speech, and mind, so also the conditions of a new existence are the results of the volitions[6] performed in previous existences. Earth, water, mountains, trees, grass, and so forth, are all born of the element of temperature and they may be quite properly be called the children or the issue of volition, or the element of kamma, as they are all born through kamma.

5. *Ekaggatā* means concentration of mind. It is also called concentration (*samādhi*). It becomes prominent in the *jhāna-samāpatti* the attainment of the supernormal modes of mind called *jhāna*.

6. *Jīvita* means the life of mental phenomena. It is pre-eminent in preserving the continuance of mental phenomena.

7. *Manasikāra* means attention. Its function is to bring the desired object into view of consciousness.

These seven factors are called common properties, as they always enter into the composition of all consciousness.

---

6 "Asynchronous volition" is the name given to it in the Paṭṭhāna, and it is known by the name of *kamma* in the actions of body, speech and mind.

The Particular Properties

8. *Vitakka* means initial application of mind. Its function is to direct the mind towards the object of investigation. It is also called *saṅkappa* (aspiration), which is of two kinds: *sammā-saṅkappa* or right aspiration, *micchā-saṅkappa* or wrong aspiration.

9. *Vicāra* means sustained application of mind. Its function is to keep the mind engaged in the object (by considering, reflecting, etc.).

10. *Viriya* means energy, or effort of mind in actions. It is of two kinds, right effort and wrong effort.

11. *Pīti* means pleasurable interest of mind, or buoyancy, or rapture of mind.

12. *Chanda* means desire-to-do, such as desire-to-go, desire-to-speak, and so forth.

13. *Adhimokkha* means decision, or literally, apartness of mind from the object; it is intended to connote the freedom of mind from the wavering state between the two courses; "Is it?" or "Is it not?"

These last six mental properties are not common to all classes of consciousness, but severally enter into their composition in some cases. Hence they are called particulars. They make thirteen if they are added to the common properties; and both, taken together, are called mixers as they enter into composition both moral and immoral consciousness.

The Immoral Properties

14. *Lobha* ethically means greed, but psychologically it means agglutination of mind with objects. It is sometimes called *taṇhā* (craving), sometimes *abhijjhā*

(covetousness), sometimes *kāma* (lust), and sometimes *rāga* (sensual passion).

15. *Dosa* in its ethical sense is hate, but psychologically it means the violent striking of mind at the object (i.e., conflict). It has two other names *paṭigha* (repugnance) and *vyāpāda* (ill-will).

16. *Moha* means dullness or lack of understanding. It is also called *avijjā* (nescience), *aññāṇa* (not knowing) and *adassana* (not seeing).

The above three are called the three immoral roots, as they are the main sources of all immorality.

17. *Diṭṭhi* means error or wrong view in matters of philosophy. It takes impermanence for permanence, non-soul for soul, and moral activities for immoral ones; or it denies that there are any results of action, and so forth.

18. *Māna* means conceit or wrong estimation. It wrongly imagines the name-and-form (*nāma-rūpa*) to be an "I," and estimates it as noble or ignoble according to the caste, creed, or family, and so on, to which the person belongs.

19. *Issā* means envy, lack of appreciation, or absence of inclination to congratulate others upon their success in life. It also means a disposition to find fault with others.

20. *Macchariya* means selfishness, meanness, or unwillingness to share with others.

21. *Kukkucca* means worry, anxiety, or undue remorse for what has been done wrongly, or for right actions that have been left undone. There are two wrongs in the world, namely, doing evil deeds and failing to do meritorious deeds. There are also two ways of repenting, thus "I have done evil acts," or "I have left undone

meritorious acts, such as charity, virtue, and so forth." "A fool always invents plans after all is over," runs the saying. So worry is of two kinds, with regard to forgetfulness and with regard to evil, "sins of omission" and "sins of commission."

22. *Ahirika* means shamelessness. When an evil act is about to be committed, no feeling of shame such as "I will be corrupted if I do this," or "Some people may know this of me," arises in him who is shameless.

23. *Anottappa* means utter recklessness as regarding such consequences as self-accusation ("I have been foolish; I have done wrong," and so forth), accusations by others, punishment in the present life inflicted by rulers, and punishment to be suffered in the realms of misery in the next life.

24. *Uddhacca* means restlessness or distraction of mind as regards an object.

25. *Thīna* means slothfulness of mind, that is, the dimness of the mind's consciousness of an object.

26. *Middha* means slothfulness of mental properties that is, the dimness of the faculties of each of the mental properties, such as contact, feeling, and so forth.

27. *Vicikicchā* means perplexity or sceptical doubt, that is, not believing what ought to be believed.

The above fourteen kinds are called *akusala-dhamma* (immoral states); in fact, they are real immoralities.

The Moral Properties

28. *Alobha* means disinterestedness of mind as regards an object. It is also called *nekkhamma-dhātu* (the element of renunciation) and *anabhijjhā* (liberality).

29. *Adosa* or amity, in its ethical sense, means incli-

nation of mind in the direction of its object, or purity of mind. It is also called *avyāpāda* (non-ill-will or peace of mind) and *mettā* (loving-kindness).

30. *Amoha* means knowing things as they are. It is also called *ñāṇa* (knowledge), *paññā* (wisdom), *vijjā* (true knowledge), *sammā-diṭṭhi* (right view).

These three are called the three moral roots as they are the main sources of all morality.

31. *Saddhā* means faith in what ought to be believed.

32. *Sati* means constant mindfulness in good things so as not to forget them.

33. *Hiri* means modesty, that is, hesitation in doing evil deeds through shame of being known to do them.

34. *Ottappa* means moral dread, that is, hesitation in doing evil deeds through fear of self-accusation, or accusation by others, or punishment in this world and in the realms of misery.

35. *Tatra-majjhattatā* is balance of mind, that is, the mode of mind which neither cleaves to an object nor repulses it. This is called *upekkhā-brahmavihāra*, equanimity of the sublime abodes, and *upekkhā-sambojjhaṅga*, equanimity that pertains to the factors of enlightenment.

36. *Kāya-passaddhi* means composure of mental properties.

37. *Citta-passaddhi* means composure of mind. Composure means that the mental properties are set at rest and have become cool, as they are free from the three immoral roots, which cause annoyance in doing good deeds.

38. *Kāya-lahutā* means buoyancy of mental properties.

39. *Citta-lahutā* means buoyancy of mind. Buoyancy means that the mental properties have become

light, as they are free from the immoral properties, which weigh against them in the doing of good deeds. It should be explained in the same manner as the rest.

40. *Kāya-mudutā* means pliancy of mental properties.

41. *Citta-mudutā* means pliancy of mind.

42. *Kāya-kammaññatā* means fitness for work of the mental properties.

43. *Citta-kammaññatā* means the fitness for work of the mind.

44. *Kāya-pāguññatā* means proficiency of the mental properties.

45. *Citta-pāguññatā* means proficiency of the mind. Proficiency here means skilfulness.

46. *Kāyujukatā* means rectitude of mental properties.

47. *Cittujukatā* means rectitude of mind.

48. *Sammā-vācā* means right speech, that is, abstinence from the four wrong modes of speech: lying, slander, abusive language, and idle talk.

49. *Sammā-kammantā* means right action, that is, abstinence from the three wrong acts: killing, stealing, and sexual misconduct.

50. *Sammā-ājīva* means right livelihood.

The above three are called the three abstinences.

51. *Karuṇā* means pity, sympathy, compassion, or wishing to help those who are in distress.

52. *Muditā* means appreciation of and delight in the success of others.

These last two are called sublime abodes (*brahma-vihāra*) and are also called illimitables (*appamaññā*).

Nibbāna

Nibbāna may be classified into three kinds:

1. Freedom or deliverance from the plane of misery is the first Nibbāna.
2. Freedom or deliverance from the world of sense-desire is the second Nibbāna.
3. Freedom or deliverance from the fine-material and the immaterial worlds is the third Nibbāna.[7]

Consciousness, the fifty-two mental properties, and Nibbāna altogether make up fifty-four mental phenomena. Thus the twenty-eight material phenomena and fifty-four mental phenomena make up eighty-two ultimate things which are called ultimate facts. On the other hand, self, soul, creature, person, and so forth, are conventional facts.

Causes I

Of these eighty-two ultimate things Nibbāna, inasmuch as it lies outside the scope of birth (*jāti*), does not need any cause for its maintenance since it also does not come within the range of decay and death (*jarā-maraṇa*). Hence Nibbāna is unconditioned and uncompounded.

---

7 The first refers to the first of the four stages of emancipation, stream-entry (*sotāpatti*), where rebirth in the lower worlds is excluded. Since, already at this stage, the final attainment of Nibbāna is assured after at most seven existences, the author calls it, in anticipation, the first Nibbāna. The second applies to the stage of the non-returner (*anāgāmi*) who has eliminated the fourth of the ten fetters, sensual lust (*kāma-rāga*). The third is the stage of Arahatship where all fetters are destroyed, among these the desire for fine-material and immaterial existence (*rūpa-* and *arūpa-rāga*).—(Ed.)

But with the exception of Nibbāna, the other eighty-one phenomena, both mental and material, being within the spheres of birth, decay, and death, are conditioned and compounded things.

Among the four causes already dealt with in connection with the material qualities, kamma is merely an originator and mind (*citta*) is simply a stimulus. The physical body develops, stands, and is maintained by the power of the heat element and by the power of the essence of nutriment. If the forces of the latter two come to an end, the forces of the former two also can no longer operate but cease simultaneously.

In the case of trees, for example, the seeds are only their origins. They grow, develop, and are maintained by the elements of earth and water. If these two principles fail them, the power of the seed also fails along with them. Here the physical body is like the tree; kamma is like the seed; the heat-element is like the earth; the nutritive essence is like the rain-water, which falls regularly at proper seasons; and mind is like the atmosphere and the heat of the sun, both of which give support from outside.

With regard to the causes of mind and mental properties, three things are needed for the arising of resultants: a past kamma, a base to depend upon, and an object. The first is like the seed of the tree, the base is like the earth, and the object is like the rain-water.

Two things are necessary for the arising of each of the mental phenomena of the moral properties, the immoral properties, and the ineffective properties, a base to depend upon, and an object. However, to be more detailed, full rational exercise of attention (*yoniso manasikāra*, or rationally-directed attention) is needed for the moral properties, and irrational exercise of attention (*ayoniso-manasikāra*, or irrationally-directed attention) for the immoral properties. The ineffective properties which have apperceptional functions have the same causes as the moral properties. As for the two classes of consciousness called "turning towards (the object)," if they precede the moral properties they have the same causes as the moral properties; if they precede the immoral properties they have the same causes as the immoral properties. Here, *yoniso-manasikāra* means proper exercise of attention and *ayoniso-manasikāra* means improper exercise of attention. These are the functions of the two classes of consciousness called *āvajjana*, "turning towards." On seeing a man, if attention is rationally utilised, moral consciousness arises; and if attention is irrationally utilised, immoral consciousness arises. There is no particular object which purely of itself will cause to arise only a moral consciousness or only an immoral consciousness. The process of the mind may be compared to a boat of which the *āvajjana-citta* or "turning-towards-thought" is the helmsman. As the course of a boat lies entirely in the hands of the helmsman, so too the occurrence of moral and immoral consciousness lies entirely in the hands of the *āvajjana-citta*.

What the seed is to the tree, that the attention is to the moral properties and the immoral properties. What the earth is to a tree, that their base is to the moral properties and immoral properties. While what the rain-water is to a tree, that their object is to the moral properties and immoral properties.

Causes II

We will now set forth the causes in another way.

Each of the six classes of consciousness has four causes.

For the arising of consciousness of sight, there is needed the eye-base, a form-object, light, and attention. Unless there is light, the function of seeing will not take place, nor the process of cognition. Attention is a name for the *āvajjana-citta*, which turns the mind towards the cognition of the form-object.

For the arising of the consciousness of sound, there is needed the ear-base, a sound-object, space, and attention. Here, space is needed for the sound to be communicated to the ear.

The function of hearing can take place only when it is present; the process of ear-door cognition also occurs only when hearing takes place.

For the arising of the consciousness of smell, there is needed the nose-base, a smell-object, air, and attention. Here, "air" means the air in the nose of the inhaled air. If this is not present, odours cannot come into contact with the nose-base, and consequently the function of smelling and the nose-base, and consequently the function of smelling and the nose-door cognition cannot take place.

For the arising of the consciousness of taste, there is needed the tongue-base, an object of taste, water, and attention. "Water" means wetness of the tongue. If the tongue is dry, the savour or sapidity cannot come into contact with the tongue-base and consequently the function of tasting and the tongue-door cognition cannot take place.

For the arising of the consciousness of touch, there is needed the body-base, an object of touch, a degree of coarseness (*thaddha*) in the object of touch, and attention.

Only a somewhat coarse object of touch can make an impression upon the body-base. If the object of the touch is too subtle, it cannot impinge upon the body-base. And unless there is impingement, neither consciousness of touch nor the body-door cognition can arise.

For the arising of the consciousness of mind, there is needed the heart-base, an object of thought, the mind-door, and attention. "Object of thought" (*dhammārammaṇa*) comprises the following: all material qualities other than the five sense objects, all mental phenomena, all ideas, and Nibbāna. The five-sense objects also can become objects of mind-consciousness but in order to set forth what is not related to the five senses, only thought-objects are mentioned here. The mind-door means the continuum of sub-consciousness (*bhavaṅga*). Though the heart-base is the place where consciousness of mind arises, since it does not possess the appropriate kind of sensuous organs, the impressions of objects cannot appear in the mind-door only.

The Two *Abhiññanas* or Super-Knowledges

Abhiññā means super-knowledge, the faculty of knowing pre-eminently beyond the knowledge of ordinary mankind. It is of two kinds, *samatha-abhiññā* and *dhamma-abhiññā*.

Samatha-abhiññā, means super-knowledge acquired by carrying out of the exercises in calm (*samatha*). It is of five different kinds:

1. *Iddhividha-abhiññā*
2. *Dibbasota-abhiññā*
3. *Cetopariya-abhiññā*
4. *Pubbenivāsa-abhiññā*
5. *Yathākammupagābhiññā*

The first is the supernormal powers of passing through the air, sinking into the earth, creating wonderful things, transforming oneself into different personalities.

The second is extreme sensitivity of hearing, as is possessed by celestial beings.

The third is the supernormal knowledge of others' thoughts.

The fourth is the supernormal knowledge of previous existences.

The fifth is the supernormal knowledge of the kamma in accordance with which living beings are thrown into the various spheres of existence; it resembles the supernormal vision possessed by celestial beings.

Dhamma-abhiññā means the insight by which are discerned all the things of ultimate truth (mentioned in the section on the truths) together with their respective characteristics, which are beyond the range of conventional truth. It is divided into three kinds:

1. *Sutamaya-ñāṇa*: knowledge acquired by learning
2. *Cintāmaya-ñāṇa*: knowledge acquired by reasoning
3. *Bhāvanāmaya-ñāṇa*: knowledge acquired by contemplation

The last of the three is again subdivided into two: (1) *anubodha-ñāṇa;* (2) *paṭivedha-ñāṇa*. Of these, the former is the triple insight into impermanence, suffering, and no-soul, or the insight into things with all their characteristics as they truly are. The latter is the supramundane knowledge of the four paths. By this knowledge, which can dispel the darkness of the defilements (*kilesa*) such as error, perplexity, and so forth, those who have attained the paths are brought into the light.

The Three *Pariññās* or Profound Knowledges

Pariññā means profound knowledge. It is of three kinds:

1. *Ñāta-pariññā*: autological knowledge (lit. knowledge of what has been understood")
2. *Tīraṇa-pariññā:* analytical knowledge
3. *Pahāna-pariññā:* dispelling knowledge

Ñāta-pariññā or Autological Knowledge

Ñāta-pariññā means a profound and accurate discernment of mental and material phenomena with all their proximate causes, and also of Nibbāna, as shown in the previous sections on the truths and the causes. It discerns things deeply by means of *dhamma-abhiññāṇa* (philosophical knowledge) in their ultimate aspects, dispelling all merely pictorial ideas or representations (*santhāna-paññatti*), such as hair of the body, and so forth. Even if all of these are not discerned, if only the Four Great Essentials out of twenty-eight material phenomena are discerned in the aforesaid manner, it may be said that the function of *ñāta-pariññā* as regards *rūpa* (form), is accomplished. As regards *nāma*, the mental side, if only four of the mental things—mind, feeling, perception, and volition—are thoroughly discerned in the aforesaid manner, it may also be said that the function of *ñāta-pariññā* as regards *nāma* is fulfilled. If Nibbāna can also be discerned as shown above, the function of *ñāta-pariññā* would be fully realised.

Tīraṇa-pariññā: the Triple Knowledge of Impermanence, Ill, and No-soul

Tīraṇa-pariññā means a profound and accurate discernment of momentary phenomena (both mental and material) with insight into rise and fall, by skilfully dissecting the continuity of mentality and materiality (*nāma and rūpa*) into momentary ultimates. It is of three kinds:

1. *Anicca-pariññā*: knowledge of impermanence
2. *Dukkha-pariññā*: knowledge of ill or suffering
3. *Anattā-pariññā*: knowledge of no-soul

Anicca-pariññā means either a perfect or a qualified knowledge of the law of death: conventional death and ultimate death. By "conventional death" we mean the kind of death concerning which we are accustomed to say, according to the conventional truth, that "to die some time is unavoidable for every living person or every living creature." By ultimate death we mean the momentary death of mental and material phenomena, which occurs innumerable times even in one day. The former neither possesses the real salient feature of impermanence, nor does it lie properly within the domain of *aniccā-pariññā*, but only of the recollection of death (*maraṇānussati*). In fact, it is only the latter, ultimate death, which exhibits the salient feature of impermanence, and lies within the domain of *anicca-pariññā*.

Dukkha-pariññā means either a perfect or a qualified knowledge of the intrinsic characteristic ill or suffering. Here ill is of two kinds:

1. *Vedayita-dukkha*: ill as painful feeling
2. *Bhayattha-dukkha*: fear-producing ill

Of these two, by *vedayita-dukkha*, bodily and mental pains are meant; and by bodily pain is meant the unbearable, unpleasant pain that comes to the various parts of the body; while mental pain means such pains as *soka* (sorrow), *parideva* (lamentation), *domanassa* (grief), and *upāyāsa* (despair), which are experienced by mind. *Bhayattha-dukkha* is that ill which falls within the sphere of *bhaya-ñāṇa* (knowledge of things as fearful) and of *ādīnava-ñāṇa* (knowledge of things as dangerous) to wit: *jāti-dukkha* (ill of birth), *jarā-dukkha* (ill of decay), *maraṇa-dukkha* (ill of death), *saṅkhāra-dukkha* (ill of conditionality), and *vipariṇāma-dukkha* (ill of changeability). The last two will be explained afterwards.

The Simile of the Dangerous Disease

Here is an illustration to show the difference between *vedayita-dukkha* and *bhayattha-dukkha*.

A man has a dangerous disease. He has to live on a simple diet, such as vegetables and fruit, so as to keep himself healthy and the disease in a subdued condition. If he takes rich food, such as poultry, fish, meat, and sweets, even though a sense of comfort and enjoyment may accompany such a dainty meal, after partaking of it he will suffer pain and indigestion for the whole day or maybe for many days, which will cause the disease to arise again in full force. The more dainty the meal is, the longer will he suffer. Now suppose that a friend of his, with a view to acquiring merit, brings him some nicely-cooked, buttered rice, fowl, fish, and meat. The man, fearing the agony of pain which he will have to undergo if he should eat the meal, has to thank his friend but decline it, telling him that the meal is too rich for him, and that should he eat it he would be sure to suffer. In this instance, the richly-prepared food is, of course, the pleasurable object, for it will probably furnish a nice savour to the palate while it is being eaten, which feeling of pleasure is called *vedayita-sukha*. But to him who foresees that it will cause him such pain as may break down his health, this same food is really an object devoid of pleasure. He shrinks from and fears it, for he knows that the better the savour the longer he must suffer; hence the pleasure his palate will derive from the food is to him a real fear-producing ill.

In the world, he who has not got rid of the error of ego and become safe against the danger of the dispersion of life (*vinipātana-bhaya*), and its passage to realms of misery, is like the aforesaid man who has the dangerous disease. The existences of men, devas, and Brahmas, and the pleasures experienced therein, are like the richly-prepared food and the feeling of pleasure derived from it. The state of being reborn in different existences after death is like the agony which the man has to suffer after the enjoyment of the food.

Here, *vedayita-dukkha* is synonymous with *dukkha-vedanā*, which is present in the *vedanā* triad of the "things conjoined with pleasant, unpleasant, and neutral feeling." *Bhayattha-dukkha* is synonymous with the truth of suffering (*dukkha-sacca*) and with dukkha as one of the intrinsic characteristics, i.e., impermanence, ill or suffering, and no-soul (*anicca, dukkha, anattā*.)

Hence, the perfect as well as the qualified knowledge of the ill inherent in the existences of men, devas, and Brahmas, including also the pleasures experienced therein, is called *dukkha-pariññā*.

Anattā-pariññā means the perfect or the qualified knowledge of mental and material phenomena as possessing the characteristic of no-soul. By this knowledge of things as no-soul, (*anatta-ñāṇa*), all the mental and material phenomena that belong to the ultimate truths are discerned as having no-soul, self, or substance. By it also is discerned the personal nature of the "person" of conventional truth. Neither are persons and creatures discerned as the soul or personality of mental and material phenomena; nor is it assumed that there exists, apart from these, a soul or personality which never dies but transmigrates from one existence to another. If this knowledge attains to its highest degree, it is called *anatta-pariññā*. The triple knowledge of impermanence, ill and no-soul is called *tīraṇa-pariññā*.

Pahāna-pariññā: Dispelling Knowledge

Pahāna-pariññā means the perfect or the qualified knowledge which dispels hallucinations. It dispels the three hallucinations of permanency (*nicca-vipallāsa*) by means of the insight acquired through the contemplation of impermanence: the three hallucinations of pleasure (*sukha-vipallāsa*) and the three hallucinations of purity (*subha-vipallāsa*), by means of the insight acquired through the contemplation of ill; and the three hallucinations of self (*attā-vipallāsa*) by means of the insight acquired through the contemplation of no-soul.[8]

Here *attā* or soul is the supposed underlying essence of a pictorial idea (*santhāna-paññatti*), and *jīva* or life is the supposed underlying essence of an aggregate-idea (*santati-paññatti*).

---

8 The three hallucinations of permanency are erroneously perceiving, thinking and viewing the impermanent as permanent. Similarly, in the case of pleasure, purity, and soul, the three hallucinations each obtain by way of erroneous perception, thought and view.—Tr. & Ed.

Of these two delusions, the former may be got rid of by a knowledge of the two kinds of truth, the ultimate and the conventional; but the latter can be got rid of only when the *anicca-pariññā,* the full knowledge of impermanence, reaches its summit.

Here, by *santati* is meant the continuum of aggregates of the same kind, and by *nānā-santati* is meant the continua of aggregates of different kinds.

This *santati* is of two kinds, mental and material. And the continuum of the material variety of aggregate is again sub-divided into four classes, namely, into those produced by kamma, by mind, by temperature, by food. Each of these four kinds of continua is liable to change if its respective causes change. When changes take place, the change of the continuum, of the kamma-produced class is not apparent but that of the mind-produced class is very apparent. In the one single act of sitting down many movements of the different parts of the body are to be observed. These movements and actions are nothing but the changes in the continua of aggregates.

The Growth, Decay, and Death of the Material Aggregates

In each aggregate there are three periods: birth, growth-and-decay, and death. In each step taken in the act of walking there are beginning, middle, and end. These are respectively birth, growth-and-decay, and death. Though we say "a step," this connotes the whole body; that is to say, the whole body undergoes change; the aggregates of the whole body undergo new births, new growth-and-decays, and new deaths. If a hundred steps or a thousand steps are taken in the course of a walk, then, a hundred or a thousand new births, new growth-and-decays, and new deaths take place in the whole body. A step may also be divided into two, the lifting-up aggregate and the laying-down aggregate of the foot. And in each single step, birth, growth-and-decay, and death must be noted. The same holds good with regard to all the postures of the body, such as standing, sitting, sleeping, stretching out, drawing in. Only, what is to be understood here is that all tired, wearied, inflammatory, irritative, inflictive, painful states are changes in the continua of aggregates produced by temperature. Both in exhaling and inhaling, beginning, middle, and end are all discernible. The phase of continuance of stability in the existence of the aggregates is immediately followed by decay which, in connection with such matter, is called exhaustion or weariness. It is produced by inflammatory and irritative matter, and through it unbearably painful feelings arise. Then, through these painful feelings, people become aware that exhaustion is present; but they do not apprehend the perpetual growth-and-decay of the continua. Weariness is indeed the name applied to the growth-and-decay of the continua of aggregates which at first spring up strongly and cheerfully, while the end of each of these aggregates is the death of the continuum (*santati-maraṇa*). In the same manner it is to be understood that there are beginning, middle, and end in every aggregate produced by laughter, smiling, gladness, joy, grief, sorrow, lamentation, groans, sobs, greed, hate, faith, love, and so forth. Also, in speaking it is obvious that every word has its beginning, its middle, and its end, which are respectively the momentary birth, growth-and-decay, and death of speech.

With regard to matter produced by temperature, aggregates arise and cease at every stroke of our fan when, in hot weather, we fan ourselves. In exactly the same way, while we are bathing there arise and cease cool aggregates each time we pour water over ourselves. Tired, fatigued, ailing aggregates, generally speaking, are changes in the temperature-produced continua. Through hot and cold foods we observe different changes in the body that are sometimes due to temperature (*utu*). The arising, aggravation, and curing of diseases by unsuitable or suitable food and medicines are also due to temperature. Even in the mind-produced aggregates, there may also be many changes which are due to temperature.

With regard to the aggregates produced by nutritive essence, poverty or abundance of flesh, vigour or defect of vital force must be taken into account. By vigour of vital force, we mean that as soon as the food taken has entered the stomach, the vital force which pervades the whole body becomes vigorous and is strengthened. Therefore, the most necessary thing for all creatures is to prevent the vital force from failing, and to promote it. What we call "getting a living in the world" is nothing else but getting regular supplies of food for the maintenance of the vital forces. If people hold that it is of great importance to remain alive, it will be obvious to them that a sufficient supply of suitable food is also a matter of great importance. It is more necessary to supply food than to increase the blood; for if the supply of food to the stomach is reduced, all blood and flesh in the body will gradually decrease. The life of the kamma-produced material qualities, such as the eye, the ear, and so forth, is the *jīvita-rūpa*, or the vital force which depends upon the supply of food. If the supply of food fails, the whole body, together with the vital force, fails. If the supply of fresh food is suspended for six or seven days, the vital force and all the kamma-produced material qualities come to an end. Then it is said that a being dies. Now, it is not necessary to indicate the changes (i.e. the birth, the growth-and-decay, and death) of the aggregates of the food-produced material qualities, for they are apparent to everyone.

The Growth, Decay, and Death of the Mental Phenomena

What has been shown is the growth-and-decay and the death of the continua of material aggregates.

Now come the continua of mental phenomena. They are also very numerous. Everyone knows his own mind. There are continua of various kinds of greed, of various kinds of hate, of various kinds of dullness, of various kinds of love. In the single act of sitting, the arising of countless thoughts is recognised by everyone. Each process of thought has its birth, decay, and death. Everyone knows of himself: "Greed is rising in me now," or "Hate is rising in me now," or "Greed has ceased in me," or "Hate has ceased in me." But it cannot be said that it has ceased forever or that it has come to its final end, for this is only the temporary cessation or death of the process or continuum of thoughts. If circumstances are favourable, they will rise again instantly. What has just been said is in exposition of the mental continuum.

Ñāta-pariññā is relevant to *tīrana-pariññā*, which in turn is relevant to *pahāna-pariññā* which is the sole necessary thing.

The Exposition of Tīraṇa-pariññā

The Mark of Impermanence in Matter

The three salient marks or features are:

1. *Anicca-lakkhaṇa*: the mark of impermanence
2. *Dukkha-lakkhaṇa*: the mark of ill or suffering
3. *Anatta-lakkhaṇa*: the mark of no-soul

Anicca-lakkhaṇa, or the mark of impermanence, is the characteristic of the sphere of *vipariṇāma* and of *aññathābhāva*. *Vipariṇāma* means metastasis, that is, a radical change in nature: a change from the present state into that which is not the present state. *Aññathābhāva* means subsequent change of mode. If the spheres of vipariṇāma and aññathābhāva are exposed to the mind's eye, it will be distinctly discerned that the mental and material phenomena which are within the spheres of these two, vipariṇāma and aññathābhāva, are really impermanent things. Therefore we have said: "*Anicca-lakkhaṇa* or the mark of impermanence, is the characteristic of the sphere of vipariṇāma and of aññathābhāva." When we closely observe and analyse the flame of a lamp burning at night, we take note of the flame together with its five salient features: birth, growth, continuance, decay, and death. We note that the fire is momentarily arising. This is the birth of a material phenomenon; but it is not fire. We observe that the flame, after arising, is constantly developing. This is the growth of the material phenomenon; but it is not fire. We observe that the flame is uninterruptedly continuing in its normal state. This is the continuance of the material phenomenon; but it is not fire. We observe that the flame is dying down.

This is the decay of the material phenomenon; but it is not fire. We observe that the flame is dying away. This is the death of the material phenomenon; but it is not fire. The property of hotness is, of course, fire. The flame quivers merely on account of the presence of these five salient features. Sometimes it may quiver when the lamp is removed, and in that case it may be said that the quivering is due to wind. These five salient features are therefore the subsequent changes (*aññathābhāva*) of the flame, called the marks of impermanence. By observing and taking note of these five salient features, it can be understood that the flame is an impermanent thing. Similarly, it should be understood that all moving things are impermanent things.

The mobile appearances of the most delicate atoms of matter, which are not discernible by the human eye, are discovered by the help of that clever revealer of nature's secrets, the microscope. Through the discovery of these moving appearances, it is believed by certain Western people—Leibnitz and Fechner, for example—that these material phenomena are living creatures. But in truth they are not living creatures, and the moving appearances are due only to the reproduction of the material phenomena through the function of the physical change (*utu*). By reproduction we here mean the *ācaya-rūpa*. In some bodies, of course, there may be living creatures in existence.

When we look at the flowing water of a river or a stream, or at the boiling water in the kettle, we discern moving appearances. These are the reproductions of material phenomena produced by physical change. And in water which seems still or quiet to the naked eye, moving appearances will also be seen with the help of a microscope. These two are reproductions of material phenomena produced by physical change. Here, "reproductions" means the constant integrations of new phenomena, which are called *ācaya-rūpas*. By discerning the integrations of new phenomena, the subsequent death or disappearances of the old phenomena, which are called the *aniccatā-rūpa*, is also discernible. When the integration of new matter and the death of the old matter take place side-by-side, the *santati-rūpa* is discernible. When the reproduction is excessive, the *apacaya-rūpa* is discernible. When the death of old matter is excessive, the *jaratā-rūpa* is discernible. We have shown above that in every tree, root, branch, leaf, sprout, flower, and fruit there are these five salient marks. So, when we look at them with the aid of a microscope, we see that they are full of very infinitesimal bodies moving about as if they were living creatures, but in fact these are mere reproductions of matter produced by physical change.

As regards the bodies of creatures or persons, these five salient marks are also discernible in every member of the body, such as hair, hair of the body, finger-nails, toe-nails, teeth, the inner skin, the outer skin, muscles, nerves, veins, big bones, small bones, marrow, kidney, heart, liver, membrane, lungs, intestines, entrails, undigested food, digested food, and the brain. So, when we look at them with the help of a microscope, moving organisms like very small creatures are seen. These are the reproductions of matter produced by kamma, mind, food, and physical change. There may, of course, be microbes in some cases. Thus, if we look with the mind's eye, the mark of impermanence in all the matter of the whole body will clearly be discerned.

What has just been expounded is the mark of impermanence in matter.

The Mark of Impermanence in Mental Phenomena

In mental phenomena, i.e., mind and its concomitants, the mark of impermanence which has two distinct features, radical change (*vipariṇāma*) and the subsequent change (*aññathābhāva*), is no less clearly to be seen. In the world, we all know that there are many different terms and expressions applied to the different modes and manners of the elements of mind and body, which are incessantly rising and ceasing. For instance, there are two expressions, "seeing" and "not-seeing," which are used in describing the function of the eye. Seeing is the term assigned to the element of sight-consciousness; or, when we say "one sees," this is the term applied in describing the arising of sight-consciousness from the conjuncture of four causes, namely, eye-base, visual form, light, and attention. And when we say, "one does not see," this is the phrase we use in describing the non-existence of sight-consciousness. When, at night in the dark, no source of light is present, sight-consciousness does not arise upon the eye-base; it is temporarily suspended. But it will arise when the light from a fire, for instance, is introduced. And when the light is put out, sight-consciousness also will again cease. As these are five salient marks present in the flame, if the light comes to be, seeing also comes to be, sight also arises. If the light develops, seeing also develops. If the light continues, seeing also continues. If the light decays, seeing also decays. And if the light ceases, then seeing also ceases. In the daytime also, these two terms "seeing" and "not-seeing" may be used. If there is no obstruction, one sees; and if there is obstruction, one does not see. As regards eye-lids, if they are opened, one sees; and if they are shut, one does not see. What has just been expounded is the vipariṇāma and aññathābhāva of sight consciousness through the occasioning cause, light. In cases where the destruction of the eye-base occurs after conception, sight-consciousness also is lost. If the visual form is taken away out of view, sight-consciousness also ceases. While sleeping, as there is no attention, sight-consciousness subsides for some time. The genesis of all classes of consciousness that take part in the process of eye-door perception is to be understood by the term "seeing"; and the subsidence of the same is to be understood by the term "not-seeing."

Similarly, in each function of hearing, smelling, tasting, and touching, a pair of expressions (existing or otherwise) is obtainable, and these must be dealt with as to their impermanency, i.e. vipariṇāma and aññathābhāva, in the same way as sight-consciousness. With regard to mind-cognition, it has many different modes, and each is apparent in its nature of vipariṇāma and aññathābhāva through the changes of the different kinds of thought. Among the mental concomitants, taking feeling for example, the changes of pleasure, pain, joy, grief, and hedonic indifference, are very evident. So also, the changes of perception, initial application, sustained application, from good to bad and vice versa, are very obvious. It may be easily noticed by anyone that in the single posture of sitting, greed, disinterestedness, hate, and amity, each arise by turns.

What has just been expounded is the impermanence of mental phenomena. So much for the mark of impermanence.

The Mark of Ill

Briefly speaking, the marks of impermanence in vipariṇāma and aññathābhāva may also be called the mark of ill, for they are to be feared by the wise in *saṃsāra*, the wheel of life. Why are they to be feared by the wise? Because, in the world, the dangers of decay and death are the dangers most to be feared. Vipariṇāma is nothing but momentary decay and death; it is the road to death, and to the dispersion of life into different spheres. All creatures remain alive without moving to another existence only because they are sustained by various methods of preservation. Vipariṇāma is also to be feared on account of the disadvantages which may fall on ourselves. *Ācaya*, *upacaya* and *santati*, the features of aññathābhāva, may also bring many disadvantages. They may establish in the physical body many kinds of disease and ailments. They may establish in the mental continuum many kinds of afflictions (*kilesa*), many kinds of hallucination, and many other disadvantages. Every material phenomenon possesses these two marks of impermanence; and also every mental phenomenon pertaining to the three realms of being has the same two marks of impermanence. Therefore the mental and material phenomena of men, devas, and Brahmas are all subject to ill. The two marks of impermanence being always present, there are approximately three different marks of ill, *dukkha-dukkhatā*, *saṅkhāra-dukkhatā*, and *vipariṇāma-dukkhatā*.

Dukkha-dukkhatā means both bodily (*kāyika*) and mental (*cetasika*) pain. *Saṅkhāra-dukkhatā* is the state of material and mental phenomena which exists only if they are always determined, conditioned, and maintained with a great deal of exertion in every existence. The existences of Brahmas have a great amount of *saṅkhāra-dukkha*. Hardly one out of a hundred, who has abandoned all sensual pleasures, renounced the world, and practised the sublime states (*brahma-vihārā*) without regard to his own life, hereafter attains the existence of a Brahmā. Though people know that such existence is a very good thing, they do not venture to practise them, for they take them to be very hard, difficult and pain-giving. When jhānas and supernormal intellections are attained, they must be maintained with great care and trouble, for if not, they are liable to be lost in a moment upon the most trifling lapse.

Vipariṇāma-dukkhatā is the state of destruction, or death occurring at any time, day or hour, whenever circumstances are favourable to it. The existences of men, devas, and Brahmas are the real ills, since they are severally subject to the said three marks of ill.

The Eleven Marks of Ill

Speaking broadly, there are eleven marks of ill :

1. *Jāti-dukkha*: ill of birth
2. *Jarā-dukkha*: ill of decay
3. *Maraṇa-dukkha*: ill of death
4. *Soka-dukkha*: ill of sorrow
5. *Parideva-dukkha*: ill of lamentation
6. *Kāyika-dukkha*: bodily ill
7. *Cetasika-dukkha*: mental ill
8. *Upāyāsa-dukkha*: ill of despair
9. *Appiya-sampayoga-dukkha*: ill due to association with enemies
10. *Piyavippayoga-dukkha*: ill due to separation from loved ones
11. *Icchā-vighāta-dukkha*: ill due to non-fulfilment of wishes

Of these, *jāti* means birth or production. It is of three kinds, *kilesajāti*: birth of defilements, *kammajāti*: birth of actions, and *vipākajāti*: birth of effects.

Of these three, *kilesajāti* is the birth or the production of defilements such as greed, hate, dullness, error, conceit, and so forth.

Vipākajāti is the birth or production of different kinds of diseases, different kinds of ailments, and different kinds of painful feelings in the body, or the production of mean and low existence such as those of birds and animals, and so forth. Among the *kilesajātis*, greed is very fierce and violent. It will rise at any time it finds favourable circumstances, like fire fed with gunpowder. When it rises, it is very difficult to suppress it by any means whatever; it will grow in volume in an instant. Hence, it is a real "ill," since it is very much to be feared by all noble beings. The like should be understood in connection with hate, dullness, and so forth, which ethically are one thousand and five hundred in number. Just as a hill which is the abode of very poisonous serpents is feared and no one dares to approach it, so also the existences of men, devas, and Brahmās are feared; and no noble beings dare approach them with the views "my self" and "my body," for they are the birth-places of the said defilements. Therefore they are real "ills" that are to be feared.

Of the *kammajāti*, immoral actions of body, speech, and thought are the development of the defilements. Therefore they are equally as fierce as the defilements. Hence this *kammajāti* is also a real "ill" to be feared by all noble ones. Just as the villages where thieves and robbers take up their quarters are feared, and good people do not venture to approach them, so also the existences of men, devas, and Brahmās are feared, and none bent on deliverance dare approach them with such views as "my self" and "my body," for they are the birth-places of the said *kammajāti*.

As to *vipākajāti*, owing to the dreadfulness of *kilesajāti* and *kammajāti*, *vipākajāti* the rebirth into the planes of misery, is likewise always a terrible thing in the revolution of existences.

Therefore, the existences of men, and so forth, to which the *vipākajāti* together with the *kilesajāti* and the kammajāti are joined, are real "ill." The moral actions and the fortunate realms furnish food for the defilements, fuel for the flames of the defilements, so that the birth of moral actions and the birth of results therefrom, are all obtainable in the *kilesajāti*. So much for *jātidukkha*, the ill of birth.

Concerning the *jarādukkha* and *maraṇadukkha*: these are the momentary decays and deaths which follow a being from the moment of conception, and are at all times ready to cause him to fall in decay, death, or unfortunate realms whenever opportunities occur. They also obtain in connection with *vipariṇāma-dukkha*: and since they dog the steps of all living beings in every existence from the moment of conception, the existences of men, devas, and Brahmas are real "ill". So much for the ills of decay and death.

The ills of sorrow, lamentation, bodily pain, mental pain, and despair always follow the existences of men and devas, ready to arise whenever an opportunity occurs. The realms of the hells and the *peta* worlds are the realms of sorrow, lamentation, pain, grief, and despair. So much for the five kinds of dukkha.

To come into contact with persons, creatures, things, or objects with which one does not wish to unite or which one does not wish even to see is the ill due to association with enemies.

Separation from persons, creatures, things, and objects which one always wishes to meet or be united with, from which one never wishes to be parted in life or by death—this is the ill due to separation from loved ones.

To strive hard, but all in vain, to obtain anything is the ill due to non-fulfillment of wishes.

These "ills" or dukkhas are very numerous and very evident, and are also frequently met with in the world. Hence the existences, of men, devas, and Brahmas are real "ills." Of these eleven varieties of dukkhas, birth, decay, and death are the most important.

So much for the mark of ill.

The Mark of No-soul

The mark by which mental and material phenomena are to be understood as no-soul is called the *anatta-lakkhaṇa*, the mark of no-soul. In considering the word *anattā*, the meaning of *attā* ought first to be understood. *Attā* in ordinary sense means essence, or substantiality. By essence or substantiality is meant, as we already explained in connection with ultimate truth, for instance the earth which is the essence or the substantiality of a pot. The word "pot" is merely the name by which is indicated a certain pictorial idea (*santhāna-paññatti*); it is not a name for earth. And a pictorial idea possesses no essence or substantiality as an ultimate thing; here earth alone is ultimate thing which possesses essence or substantiality. If the question is asked: "Does such a thing as pot exist in the world?" those who are unable to differentiate between the two kinds of truth, ultimate and conventional, would answer that the pot exists. These should then be asked to point out the pot. They will now point to an earthen pot near at hand, saying: "Is not that a pot?" But it is not correct of them to assert that earth is pot; it is a false assertion. Why is it a false assertion? Simply because earth is an ultimate thing and has essence or substantiality, while pot is a mere conception having no essence or substantiality, and thus, like space, is void. To assert of earth that it is pot is in effect to try to make out that essential earth constitutes the essence or substantiality of the pot, which is actual fact, seeing that pot as a mere representation of the mind possesses that no substantial essence whatever. Here, what actually is non-existent pot becomes existent pot, and earth also becomes attā of the pot, so that earth and pot become one and the same thing; the identity of the one is confused with the identity of the other. It is for this reason that we call this a false assertion. In this illustration, earth corresponds to the five aggregates or their constituents, material and mental phenomena, while pot corresponds to persons and living creatures. Just as earth becomes the essence of pot in the statement that the earth is the pot, so also the five aggregates or their constituents become the attā or the essence of persons and creatures, when it is said that the aggregates are persons and creatures. This is the meaning of attā.

Now for *anattā*. In the expression "earthen pot," if one is able to discern that earth is one thing and pot another, and that earth is an ultimate thing and pot a mere conception of the mind; and again, that earth is not pot and pot is not earth, and also that it is false to call earth a pot, and to call pot earth; then the earth becomes not the essence or attā of the pot, but becomes anattā, void of essence; at the same time, the pot is seen to be void like space, since it is a mere conception of form. A like result is obtained if one is able to discern the five aggregates and the material and mental phenomena thus: The five aggregates are ultimate things; persons and creatures are ideas derived from their forms and continua; hence the phenomena are not persons and creatures; and persons and creatures are not the phenomena. If the phenomena are called persons and creatures, this is a false naming of them; and if persons and creatures are called the phenomena, this is false too. Accordingly, the phenomena become not the essence of persons and creatures, but become anattā, or the reverse of substantial essence. Also, persons and creatures become quite evidently void and empty, inasmuch as they are mere ideas derived from the forms and continua of the phenomena. What has just been said is in exposition of the meaning of anattā.

How the Marks of Impermanence and Ill Become Marks of No-soul

The marks of impermanence and ill expounded in the foregoing pages are also the marks of no-soul. How? It is supposed that the ideas (*paññatti*) of persons and creatures are eternal and immortal[9] both in this existence

---

9 In Buddhist philosophy there are three things which are "eternal and immortal," in the sense in which that phrase is used here in the text. These three things are, in Pāli, *paññatti, ākāsa,* and *nibbāna*; that is, concepts (or ideas), space, and that which supervenes when craving, hate and delusion are completely wiped out. It is held that the existence of these three has nothing whatever to do with time, never enters time, is never limited by time. The law of rise-and-fall, of arising and ceasing, which applies to all other things, does not apply to them. They exist independent of whether any particular being thinks them or not. In other words, they are eternal and immortal and independent of time, not in any sense of being unbrokenly continuous in time. Nibbāna is

and in those that follow, and it has been explained that the phenomena are not eternal since they are subject to momentary decay and death which are the marks of impermanence; and also because they are constantly ceasing and being reproduced innumerable times even in one day, the mark of that kind of impermanence is known as aññathābhāva.

But in the ideas of persons and creatures no marks of radical change (*viparināma*) and subsequent change (*aññathābhāva*) are to be seen. If such marks were to be found in the ideas of persons and creatures, then, of course, these ideas would also be subject to birth, decay, and death, and would be reborn and decay and die many times even in one day. But these marks are not to be found in the ideas; we discern these marks only in the mental and material phenomena. Therefore it comes to this, that the mental and material phenomena (*nāma-rūpa-dhammā*) are not to be regarded as the essence or substantiality of persons and creatures. It is in this way that the mark of impermanence becomes the mark of no-soul, in accordance with the text: *asārakatthena anattā*, "On account of being without a core, the word anattā is used."

How does the mark of ill become the mark of no-soul? The marks of ill are very evil, very disadvantageous, and very unsatisfactory; and all creatures desire to be in good states, to be prosperous, and to be satisfied. If mental and material phenomena are the true essence of persons and creatures, the phenomena and the person

---

distinguished from the two other "eternal and immortal" things in that it has *santilakkhaṇa* or it is *santibhāva*, a word which may be rendered quite adequately in English as "the great peace" and all that this implies.—Translator.

must be one and the same. And if this be so, their desires must also be one and the same; that is, the person's desire must also be that of the phenomena, and vice-versa. But if this is not so, then each must be a thing separate from the other.

Here, by a "person's desire" we mean greed (*lobha*) and desire-to-do (*chanda*); and by "the desire of phenomena," the happening of things in accordance with their causes. A main characteristic of persons and creatures is the craving for happiness of mind and body; and an outstanding feature of phenomena is their uniformity with their causes or conditions, that is, the arising and the ceasing of phenomena are subject to causes, and never occur entirely in accordance with the desires of persons in defiance of causes. For example: if warmth is wanted, the cause that produces warmth must be sought out; or if coldness is wanted, the cause that produces coldness must be sought out. If long life is wanted, the causes of long life, for instance, a daily supply of suitable food, must be sought out; for no man can live long merely by wishing to live long. And if rebirth in the worlds of the fortunate is wanted, then the cause of this, moral or virtuous deeds, must be sought out; for no one can get to the worlds of the fortunate merely by wishing to be reborn there.

It is sometimes erroneously believed that one can be whatever one wishes to be, because upon occasions something one has wished for is later on fulfilled. But in actual fact it has come about only in accordance with a cause that was previously sought out and brought into play. It is falsely believed by many people that one can maintain oneself according to one's wish when in sound health or at ease in any of the four bodily postures, ignoring the fact that the cause, the partaking of food on previous days, was sought by them and brought into play. They also mistakenly think that their wishes are always fulfilled, when they find themselves living happily in buildings previously in existence. But in truth, if one looks around in this world and sees how great and numerous are the businesses, affairs, occupations and so forth, of men in all their extent and variety, he will soon discern with the mind's eye that the *saṅkhāra-dukkha*, the suffering associated with conditioned phenomena, is great and manifold in precisely the same measure as men's activities. And this dukkha is due to the establishing of the causes necessary for acquiring of the desired effects; for the phenomena can never become exactly as beings wish them to be or order them to be. Thus, simply in beholding the marks of *saṅkhāra-dukkhatā* all about us, it becomes evident that phenomena do not spontaneously conform to the desires of persons and creatures, and hence they are not their essence or substance. In addition to this, it also should be well noted how conspicuous is non-substantiality with regard to the other types of ill aforementioned, as *dukkha-dukkhatā, vipariṇāma-dukkhatā, jāti-dukkha, jarā-dukkha, maraṇa-dukkha,* and so forth.

So much for the mark of no-soul from the standpoint of ill or suffering.

The Three Knowledges pertaining to Insight of the Three Marks

The three knowledges pertaining to the insight that fully grasps the meaning of the three marks are called *tīraṇa-pariññā*.

These three knowledges pertaining to the insight are:

1. *Anicca-vipassanā-ñāṇa*: insight-knowledge in contemplating impermanence
2. *Dukkha-vipassanā-ñāṇa*: insight-knowledge in contemplating ill
3. *Anattā-vipassanā-ñāṇa*: insight-knowledge in contemplating no-soul

Of these three knowledges, the last-mentioned must be acquired primarily and fully in order to dispel the error of the soul doctrine. And in order to obtain fully this last-mentioned knowledge, the first must be introduced; for, if the first is well discerned, the last is easily acquired. As for the second, it does not culminate through the acquisition of the first. It is owing to imperfection in obtaining the second knowledge that the transcendental path has four grades, and that lust and conceit are left undispelled. Hence the most important thing for Buddhists to do is to free themselves entirely from the ills of the realms of misery (*apāyadukkha*), i.e., the suffering experienced through rebirth in subhuman worlds. There is no way of escaping from them open to men when the teachings of the Buddha vanish from the world. To escape from the ills of unhappy rebirths means to put away all immoral actions and erroneous views, and to put away all erroneous views means to put away utterly the view of soul. Therefore, in this life in which we are so fortunate to encounter the teaching of the Buddha, we should strive to contemplate or meditate upon the impermanence of things, and thus to bring to fullness the insight-knowledge of no-soul. In confirmation of this, here is a quotation from the texts:

> To him, O Meghiya, who comprehends impermanence, the comprehension of no-soul manifests itself. And to him who comprehends no-soul, the fantasy of an 'I' presiding over the five aggregates is brought to destruction; and even in this present life he attains Nibbāna.

There is no need for us to expatiate upon the truth of this text, for we have already shown how the mark of impermanence can become the mark also of no-soul.

The insight exercises can be practised not only in solitude, as is necessary in the case of the exercise of calm or *samatha*, but they can be practised everywhere. Maturity of knowledge is the main thing required. For if knowledge is ripe, the insight of impermanence may easily be accomplished while listening to a discourse or while living a householder's ordinary life. To one whose knowledge is developed, everything within and without oneself, within and without one's house, within and without one's village or town, is an object at the sight of which the insight of impermanence may spring up and develop. But those whose knowledge is, so to speak, still in its infancy, can accomplish this only if they practise assiduously the exercises in calm.

Consideration of the momentary deaths which occur innumerable times even during the wink of an eye is only required in discussion on Abhidhamma. But in meditating or practising the exercises in insight, all that is needed is consideration of the *santati-vipariṇāma* and the *santati-aññathābhāva*, that is, of the radical change and sequent change of the continua, things which are evident to and personally experienced by every man alive.

The exercises in insight that ought to be taken up are, first, the four great elements from among the material qualities, and the six classes of cognition from among the mental qualities. If one can discern the arising and ceasing of the four elements innumerable times in one day alone, the changes, arisings, and ceasings of the derivative material qualities are also discerned. Of the mental qualities also, if the changes of consciousness are discerned, those of the mental concomitants are simultaneously discerned. In particular, the conspicuous feelings, perceptions, volitions, and so forth, from among the mental qualities, and the conspicuous forms, odours, and so forth from among the material qualities may be taken as objects for the exercise, as they will quickly enable a meditator to acquire with ease the insight of impermanence.

However, from the philosophical point of view, the insight is acquired in order to dispel such notions as "creatures," "persons," "soul," "life," "permanence," "pleasures," and to get rid of the hallucinations. The acquisition of insight also mainly depends on a sound grasp of the three marks, which have been sufficiently dealt with already.

So much for the exposition of *tīraṇapariññā*.

The Exposition of Pahāna-pariññā

The Five Kinds of Dispelling

In Buddhist teachings there are five kinds of *pahāna*, i.e. the dispelling, putting away or giving up of mental defilements:

1. *Tadaṅga-pahāna*: the temporary dispelling of the defilements by substitution of the opposite
2. *Vikkhambhana-pahāna*: the temporary dispelling by suppression in the jhānas
3. *Samuccheda-pahāna*: the eradication of defilements effected at the moment of attaining the paths (*magga*) of emancipation (*sotāpatti-magga*, etc.)
4. *Paṭippassaddhi-pahāna*: the tranquillisation of defilements at the fruition-stage (*phala*) of emancipation (*sotāpatti-phala*, etc.)
5. *Nissaraṇa-pahāna*: the final escape or deliverance from the defilements on attaining Nibbāna

In order to make clear these five kinds of *pahāna*, the three periods or stages (*bhūmi*) must be mentioned here. They are:

1. *Anusaya-bhūmi*: the stage of latency, the inherent tendency for defilements
2. *Pariyuṭṭhāna-bhūmi*: the stage of mental involvement or obsession through the occurrence of defiled thought processes
3. *Vītikkama-bhūmi*: the stage of actual transgression in words or deeds.

Of these three, *anusaya-bhūmi* is the period during which the defilements lie latent surrounding the life-continuum (*bhavaṅga*), but have not come into existence as thought processes within the three phases of time.

Pariyuṭṭhāna-bhūmi is the period during which the defilements rise from the latent state and manifest themselves as thought processes at the mind-doors when any object that has the power to arouse them produces a perturbation at any of the six doors of perception.

Vītikkama-bhūmi is the period at which the defilements become so fierce and ungovernable that they produce evil actions in deed and word. Thus, during repeated existences without known beginning, every occurrence of greed that goes along with a being's life-continuum has these three periods. Similarly, all other defilements, like hate, ignorance, conceit, etc., have three periods each.

There are three kinds of training (*sikkhā*) in Buddhism, namely: the training of morality (*sīla*), in concentration (*samādhi*), and in wisdom (*paññā*). The training in morality is able to dispel only the third stage of the defilements, that of actual transgression. As there remain two stages undispelled, the defilements temporarily put away by morality can arise again and soon fill up until they reach the stage of transgression.

The second training, in concentration, through attaining the first jhāna, the second jhāna, and so forth, is able to dispel only the second stage of the defilements left undispelled by morality, that is, the mental involvement by evil thought process. As the stage of latency is still undispelled, if obstacles to jhāna were encountered, the defilements temporarily put away by jhāna would soon arise and grow until they reach the stage of transgression. Therefore the dispelling by concentration is called *vikkhambhana-pahāna*, which means the putting away to a distance by suppression. Here jhāna can dispose of the defilements for a considerable time so that they do not arise soon again, for meditation is more powerful in combating the defilements than morality.

The third training, the training in wisdom—the knowledge that belongs to insight and the knowledge that pertains to the supramundane path—is able to dispel the first, latent stage of the defilements left undispelled by morality and concentration. The defilements that are entirely got rid of through wisdom, leaving nothing behind, will never rise again. Therefore the putting away by wisdom that has reached the supramundane paths of stream-entry, etc., is called dispelling by eradication (*samuccheda-pahāna*). The knowledge that pertains to supramundane fruition puts the defilements away by tranquillising the same defilements that have been put away by the knowledge that pertains to the supramundane path, this putting away is called the *paṭippassaddhi-pahāna*. The putting away by entering Nibbāna is called the *nissaraṇa-pahāna*, the utter escape from the ties of existence forever.

Now, we have seen that knowledge is of three kinds: knowledge of insight, knowledge pertaining to the supramundane path, and knowledge pertaining to supramundane fruition. Of these, though the knowledge of insight is able to put away the first, latent stage of the defilements (*anusaya-bhūmi*), it is not able to put it away completely. Only the knowledges pertaining to the paths are able to put away all the defilements that respectively belong to each path. The knowledge pertaining to *sotāpatti-magga*, the first path, utterly dispels and eradicates all erroneous views and perplexities. It also finally dispels all immoral actions that could result in rebirth in the realms of misery. The knowledge pertaining to *sakadāgāmi-magga*, the second path, dispels all coarse lust and hate. The knowledge pertaining to *anāgāmi-magga*, the third path, dispels all subtle lust and ill-will, left undispelled by the second path. To the *anāgāmi* or never-returner, the link of kinship with this world is broken, and the Brahmā world is the only sphere where he may take rebirth. The knowledge pertaining to *arahatta-magga*, the fourth path, dispels the defilements which were left undispelled by the lower paths. One who kills all defilements becomes an Arahat and escapes from the three worlds. In our Buddhist religion, the dispelling by eradication is the chief thing to be accomplished.

So much for the *pahāna-pariññā*.

The Practice of Insight Meditation

I will now indicate the main points necessary to those who practise the exercises of insight. Of the three knowledges of insight, the knowledge of impermanence must first and foremost be acquired. How? If we carefully watch the cinematograph show, we will see how quick are the changes of the numerous series of photographs representing the wonderful scene, all in a moment of time. We will also see that a hundred or more photographs are required to represent the scene of a moving body. These are, in fact, the functions of *viparināma* and *aññathābhāva*, or the representation of impermanence or death, or cessation of movements. If we carefully examine the movements in a scene, such as the walking, standing, sitting, sleeping, bending, stretching, and so forth, of the parts of the body during a moment of time, we will see that these are full of changes, or full of impermanence. Even in a moment of walking, in a single step, there are numerous changes of pictures which may be called impermanence or death. It is also the same with the rest of the movements. Now, we must apply this to ourselves. The impermanence and the death of mental and material phenomena are to be found to the full in our bodies, our heads, and in every part of the body. If we are able to discern clearly those functions of impermanence and death which are always operating in our bodies, we shall acquire the insight of the destruction (*bhaṅga-ñāṇa*), into the breaking-up, falling-off, cessation, and changes of the various parts of the body in each second, in each fraction of a second. That is, we shall discern the changes of every part of the body, small and great, of head, of legs, of hands, and so forth. If this be thus discerned, then it may be said that the exercise on the contemplation of impermanence is well accom–plished. And if the exercise on the contemplation of impermanence is well accomplished, then that of the contemplation of non-soul is also accomplished. If this is thus discerned, then it may be said that the exercise on the contemplation of impermanence is well accom–plished. By the word "accomplished," it is meant that the exercise has been properly worked out so as to remain a permanent possession, during the whole term of life; but it is not meant that the knowledge of the path and of fruition has been attained. The attainment of the knowledge of the path and fruition, however, is quick or slow, according to opportunity or lack of opportunity in the practice of higher virtues.

It is also very difficult to become correctly aware of the attainment of the paths and of the fruits. In fact, even the *ariya* who has attained the first path hardly knows that he has become an attainer of the stream-of-the-path. Why? Because of the unfathomableness of the latent stage of the defilements. Those yogis or meditators who do not know the unfathomableness of the latent stage of the defilements, sometimes think themselves to be attainers of the stream-of-the-path while as yet their erroneous views and perplexity are only partially, but not completely, put away. If error and perplexity, with all their latent states, are eradicated by the *samuccheda-pahāna*, they would become the real attainers of the stream-of-the-path. The meditators or practisers of insight, however, for the whole term of life, must gladly continue in the exercise on the contemplation of impermanence until the exercise is systematically worked out. Even the Arahants do not give up these exercises for the securing of tranquillity of mind. If meditators practise these exercises for the whole term of life, their knowledge will be developed till they pass beyond the *puthujjana-bhūmi*, the stage of the worldling, and arrive at the *ariya-bhūmi*, the stage of the noble ones, either before death or at the time of death, either in this life or in the life following, in which latter case they will be reborn as devas.

Conclusion

Here the concise *Vipassanā Dīpanī, The Manual of Insight*, written for the Buddhists of Europe, comes to a close. It was written in Mandalay, while I was sojourning in the Ratanasiri Monastery, where the annual meeting of the Society for Propagating Buddhism in Foreign Countries took place; and it was finished on the 14th waxing of Taboung in the year 2458 B.E., corresponding to the 26th February, 1915 C. E.

The Noble Eightfold Path and Its Factors Explained

(Maggaṅga-dīpanī)

The Noble Eightfold Path and Its Factors Explained

(Maggaṅga-dīpanī)

The Venerable Ledi Sayadaw

Translated into English by

U Saw Tun Teik

Revised edition by

Bhikkhu Khantipālo

Introduction

If a Buddhist is asked, "What did the Buddha teach?" he would rightly reply, "The Four Noble Truths and the Noble Eightfold Path." If he is then questioned further as to what they consisted of, he should be able to define them accurately, without uncertainty, ambiguity, or recourse to his own ideas.

This is very important—that the supremely clear words of the Buddha are not distorted, either through ignorance or because of one's own speculations. The Buddha has often praised deep learning, just as he has pointed out the dangers in holding opinions and views which are the result only of one's personal feelings and preferences, or of misinterpreted experience. There is little to excuse such things since the Buddha himself has carefully defined what is meant by the truth of *dukkha* (suffering), or what constitutes right view, just to take two examples.

The Buddha's definitions are unconfusing while convincing since they arise from his Unsurpassed Perfect Awakening. But one's own ideas, or the speculations of those who depart from his words, cannot be so without some bias towards what is more comforting to believe, what, in other words, one's undisciplined emotions draw one to believe (see note 41). Such "tangles of views" are endless in this world and produce much conflict as well. No good comes of holding views.

Those who do so usually do not like to practice the Dhamma; they prefer to think about it and talk about it. But one does not become a Buddhist by mere thinking and talking, only by *practice*, and this Noble Eightfold Path containing within it the Four Noble Truths is the pre-eminent path of practice—of wisdom, moral conduct, and meditation.

So here is a booklet where the Buddha's own definitions of the Four Noble Truths and the Path are quoted and explained by the venerable author who, as a senior member of the Sangha (Order) in Burma, was both deeply learned and well practiced in meditation. This handbook of the Noble Eightfold Path contains all the path-factors clearly described according to the most ancient Buddhist tradition, which has come down to us from the enlightened disciples of the Buddha to the great teachers of the present day in the Buddhist countries of Southeast Asia.

Now it only remains to thoroughly learn the definitions of the path-factors and, of course, to practice them. Then one will be competent to answer questions convincingly since one's own conduct does not depart from Dhamma.

This work was written by the Venerable Mahāthera Ledi Sayādaw in Burmese and was later translated into English by U Saw Tun Teik, an advocate in Rangoon. The Union Buddha Sāsana Council issued this book after revision by their English Editorial Board in 1961, but due to later events in Burma it has long been hard to find.

In making it available once again this opportunity has been taken to rewrite it in a form more easily read by Western people, omitting most of the Pāli words which are found in the first edition. Venerable Nyāna-ponika Mahāthera encouraged me to take up this work, gave every helpful advice, and sent me his copy of the first edition to work on. Also, some sections from the venerable author's *Sammādiṭṭhi-dīpanī* (*The Manual of Right View*) have been included in the revised edition. In places where the venerable author's explanations are too brief some expansions of his statements have been added by the editor. The footnotes are also mine unless stated otherwise.

Finally, if any error has been made by me during revision, may the translators pardon me, and the venerable author show me his compassion.

May the Dhamma of the Exalted One lighten the darkness of the world!

Bhikkhu Khantipālo
Forest Hermitage
Vassāna BE 2520/CE 1976

Preface

In compliance with the requests of the Englishmen who have entered the Buddhist Order of Monks for elucidation of the Noble Eightfold Path, the Venerable Ledi Sayādaw made use of his relative respite while journeying by rail or steamer from town to town, to write this treatise.[1]

---

1 This Preface was translated from Burmese and sent to the reviser by Myanuang U Tin, who has also supplied valuable information on some difficult points from his own knowledge and from replies elicited from Venerable Mahasi Sayadaw.

The Noble Eightfold Path and Its Factors Explained

Namo tassa Bhagavato Arahato Sammā-sambuddhassa
Homage to the Exalted One, the Holy One,
the Perfectly Enlightened One

This is the Noble Eightfold Path:

1. Right view — Sammā-diṭṭhi
2. Right thought—Sammā-saṅkappa
3. Right speech—Sammā-vācā
4. Right action—Sammā-kammanta
5. Right livelihood—Sammā-ājīva
6. Right effort—Sammā-vāyāma
7. Right mindfulness —Sammā-sati
8. Right concentration—Sammā-samādhi.

I. Right View

Three kinds of right view have been distinguished:

(A) That one is the owner of the kamma[2] one makes.

(B) That one has right view in respect of ten subjects concerned with kamma, its fruits, this world, other worlds, and the superknowledge revealing them.

(C) That one has right view regarding the Four Noble Truths.

---

2 *Kamma* (or in Sanskrit, *karma*) means intentional actions by body, speech, or mind, having an inherent tendency to bear fruit in accordance with the kind of action done.

First we shall examine:

A. Right View on the ownership of one's kamma

About this the Buddha has said:

> "All beings are the owners of their kamma, heirs to their kamma, born of their kamma, related to their kamma, abide supported by their kamma; whatever kamma they shall do, whether good or evil, of that they will be the heirs."

Now to take this passage section by section for a fuller understanding.

1. All beings are the owners of their kamma

This is the correct understanding that only two things, the wholesome and the unwholesome deeds done by beings, really belong to them and always accompany them on their wanderings in the wheel of birth and death.

Though people call gold, silver, wealth, and jewels their own since they have acquired them lawfully or otherwise, really they are owners only for the brief span of this life and sometimes not for as long as that. For the things that are "owned" by us must be shared with other forces and beings such as water, fire, rulers, thieves, and enemies which, if sentient, may also regard those things as their own.[3] So such things are as though borrowed for

3 Venerable Buddhaghosa in his *Path of Purification*, emphasizes that even our own body must be shared with beings, i.e. with such parasites as worms or bacteria, which regard it as their own. "Ownership" of any material thing is very tenuous and insecure.

this life, just for use now but to be given up at death. And however little or much one may own of things here, all have to be relinquished at the time of death and cannot be taken with one. When this is taken into account, we may understand how we hardly own such things at all, while by contrast the good and evil done by us is truly owned and such kamma may accompany us through a continuity of lives extending through hundreds of thousands of world-cycles in the future. Kamma cannot be taken from the doer or destroyed in any way, for it is imprinted on our minds and will bear fruit when conditions permit. Hence the Buddha has said, *"All beings are the owners of their kamma."*

One should therefore love and esteem *good conduct* more than one's own life and preserve it well, while one should dread evil conduct more than the danger of death and so refrain from evil deeds.

The kamma which is one's own consists in the mental, verbal, and physical intentional actions that one has done. Kamma by way of the body means intentional movements of such parts of the body as hands or legs. Verbal kamma includes expressions made with the mouth, tongue, and throat. Mental kamma covers all intentional functions of the mind. In the Buddha's teaching these three are called kamma.[4]

All beings make these three kinds of kamma while they are awake, and whatever work they do, of great significance or little, is all done in these three ways. But when a person is asleep these three kinds of kamma are not made, for at that time states of mind are not volition-

---

4 Note that kamma means action, *not* the fruit of action as when people say, "It's my kamma." This reduces the teaching of kamma to mere fatalism.

al. In the case of one who is dead none of the three kinds of kamma are made by that body.

These three may be analyzed as to whether they are (1) good or wholesome, or (2) evil and unwholesome; further as to whether (1) they have results ripening in this life, or (2) have them ripening in a future life.

Kamma is determined to be good or evil according to whether it leads to the cultivation and growth of one's own mind and the benefit of others, or to the deterioration and defilement of one's own mind and the harm of others. Thus by doing the following ten types of deeds one makes evil or unwholesome kamma which will bear the fruits of suffering, but by abstaining from these ten and cultivating their opposites one makes good kamma which will bear the fruits of happiness. These ten are as follows:

(1) Injuring and killing living beings (2) Stealing (3) Wrong conduct in sexual pleasures	Evil kamma by body
(4) False speech (5) Tale-bearing (6) Harsh talk (7) Useless chatter	Evil kamma by speech[5]
(8) Covetousness (9) Ill will (10) Wrong view	Evil kamma by mind

All kinds of actions done through the "three doors" of body, speech, and mind, that are free of these ten ways of making unwholesome kamma, whether in connection

5 These will be explained under right speech.

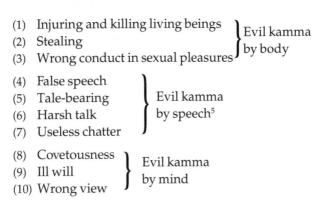

with livelihood, the acquisition of wealth, and the search for knowledge, are good kamma made in the present existence and coming to fruition now. But those actions by way of the three doors which are involved with the above ten, in whatsoever connection they are done, are evil kamma which bears its fruit in the present life.

In a similar way kammas made in this life and due to ripen in the future will also be of two kinds, either wholesome or unwholesome. Whether the wholesome kamma is made by the body, speech, or mind in connection with such actions as almsgiving, Uposatha-day observance, moral conduct (of the Five Precepts), practicing meditation, going for refuge to and paying respects to the Triple Gem, etc., they will ripen in the future, giving rise to a favorable birth.[6]

Unwholesome kammas made in this life but ripening in the future will result in birth in the lower planes of existence (as ghost, animal, or hell-wraith).

In this way one should differentiate between good and evil kamma as well as contemplate the three kinds of kamma which are made everywhere—on land, in water, and in the sky. When we have seen with our own eyes how all beings, wherever they are, have been making the three kinds of kamma in all their past existences through endless world-cycles, we can comprehend that they will make them in the future too. And just as in this world system, so there are in all directions an infinite number of other world systems where such beings, living on land, in water, and in the sky, also make the three kinds of kamma.

---

6 The Uposatha day, which falls on the days of the full moon and the new moon, is the Buddhist observance day. The Triple Gem is the Buddha, the Dhamma, and the Sangha.

When one has thought about this, it becomes clear that all these beings are living by the three kinds of kamma which they make individually for themselves. By making wholesome kamma in these ways they enjoy the fruits of happiness, while by making evil kamma in these three ways they encounter various kinds of misery and suffering.

So the three kinds of kamma made by body, speech, and mind are truly the property owned by beings, for kamma can never be destroyed by fire, water, thieves, and so on. Though a person may own nothing, not even a single coin, yet he can achieve happiness if he has made mental kamma connected with knowledge and wisdom.

Hence the Buddha declared: *"All beings are the owners of their kamma."*

Now let us take an example which illustrates the results of kamma made in the present life. People who wish for worldly gain, such as wealth, government position, or honor in this life, can fulfil their desires if they make an effort to acquire education and knowledge. If such wishes were merely a matter of worship of some God without any effort being needed, then there would be no need for the worshippers of God to engage in trading, farming, or learning arts or sciences. It would be enough just to worship God. But in fact that is not the case, for like Buddhists, Christians and Muslims also make the three kinds of kamma and caused by it they acquire worldly gain. It is not God but the three kinds of kamma which have given them these things.

Similarly, we can understand how past kamma bears fruit in the present life. For while worldly gains in this life are kamma-produced and not due to any supernatural favor, so the benefits of being reborn in a wealthy family or in a heavenly world are not God-given either, but depend on the power of kamma, such as almsgiving and purity of the moral precepts practiced in former lives. One who is reborn into a wealthy family becomes the owner of the riches there, so that all his possessions are due to his past kamma.

Here there is an analogy with vegetative growth. It is usually said that the growth and form of plants depends on the seed. But according to the Abhidhamma, the element of kinetic energy (*tejo*), classified as material change (*utu*), is the cause. The seed is just this element, and it is this which can be called the real seed. In the same way all beings have kamma as their seeds of becoming (or existence): wholesome kamma such as almsgiving, moral conduct, and the like, and unwholesome kamma such as destroying living beings, and so on.

The process of becoming variously men or animals is due to the kamma made in past existences. Having made wholesome kamma, beings are reborn as men or as gods (*deva*), while it is because of making unwholesome kamma that they obtain birth in the four lower worlds: hell (*niraya*), animals, ghosts (*peta*), and titans (*asura*).

From the seeds produced by old plants, a new generation of plants grows so that seeds from a tree and trees from seeds appear successively: a cycle of seeds and trees. Similarly, beings have planted kamma-seeds in their past existences and from these seeds new existences spring up. Thus beings make kamma which in turn gives rise successively to new states of existence.

But here we have to notice a difference between the example in this simile and the case of living beings. A tree is only a stream of material events (without a mental stream or consciousness)[7] and from one tree many fruits

7 Trees and plants have only the life faculty (*jīvitindriya*),

may be produced, from which in turn many trees may grow. In the case of beings, however, there are both mental and material streams of events of which the mental ones are chief. Though during life (as with trees) many progeny may be produced, one body giving rise to many others, the stream of mental factors continues with one mental factor giving rise to one other.

Thus at death the last moment of consciousness gives rise to the rebirth-linking consciousness of the next life. Therefore, although a being has planted many seeds of both wholesome and unwholesome kamma in one existence, one moment of volition (*cetanā* = kamma) alone produces one other resultant moment in the next existence.[8] As there is only the production of one mental factor (the first moment of consciousness at conception or spontaneous birth) so at the time of death the continuity or stream of the past material body gives rise to only one new body-stream, not more than this.

Just as earth, water, sun, moon, and stars, come into existence from the seeds of kinetic energy included in material change and were not created by a God, so such beings as men and animals come to successive existences

---

which is material. They have no consciousness and so are not part of the cycle of rebirth. Some recent books (*The Secret Life of Plants*, for example) propound theories and offer evidence that plants can sense. In some cases this could be accounted for by the presence of a tree-spirit (*rukkha-deva*) or dryad.

8 It might be objected here that a little time spent making wholesome kamma (as in the cases of Anāthapiṇḍika and Visākhā) is still producing centuries of good results, or a short while producing unwholesome kamma (as with Devadatta) brings centuries of pain, but the author is pointing out the strict sequence of events at the time of death, when one kamma at the end of life produces only one resultant moment, the rebirth-linking consciousness.

because of the seeds of their past kamma made in previous lives, even in previous world cycles. A view such as this is known as right view (*sammā-diṭṭhi*).

But to hold that a God creates beings is a wrong view, and it is the wrong view of those who, not knowing fully the operative power of kamma and material change, imagine that they were created by a God. Hence the Buddha, whose purpose was to make people abandon wrong view and to rely instead upon kamma, knowledge, and wisdom, said: "*All beings are the owners of their kamma.*"

Further as exposition of "ownership of kamma" the following objection and reply is appropriate.[9]

Question: "Well, friend, if it is true that the Supreme Buddha had properly refuted the view 'all that is experienced is rooted in past kamma,'[10] why and for what reason did he declare the following in the Subha Sutta (or Cūḷakammavibhaṅga Sutta, Majjhima Nikāya No. 135): 'Beings are the owners of their kamma, young man, heirs to their kamma, born of their kamma, related to their kamma, abide supported by their kamma. Beings are divided by kamma, that is to say, among low or excellent existences'?"

Reply: This may be answered in three ways.

(1) Those who hold the view "all that is experienced is rooted in past kamma" (*pubbekatahetu-diṭṭhi*) maintain that all pleasures and sufferings experienced by beings in the present life are conditioned and caused only by the volitional actions (*kamma*) done by them in their past exis-

---

9 This passage up to the end of this section is taken from *Samma-diṭṭhi-dīpanī, The Manual of Right View*.

10 For this view, see *Aṅguttara Nikāya Anthology*, Part I (BPS Wheel No. 155/158), pp.43–44.

tences. They reject all present causes such as energy and wisdom. As this view rejects all present causes it is known as the "one-sided base opinion" (*ekapakkhahīna-vāda*), "one-sided" because it ignores present kamma.

(2) Those who hold the "creation rooted in God view" (*issaranimmāna-hetu-diṭṭhi*) maintain that all pleasures and sufferings experienced by beings in the present life are created by a Supreme Brahma or God. They reject all past and present kamma made by beings; so their view is called the "both-sided base opinion" (*ubhayapakkhahīnavāda*), "both-sided" because it ignores both past and present kamma.

(3) Those who hold the "no cause no condition view" (*ahetu-appaccaya-diṭṭhi*) maintain that all pleasures and sufferings experienced by beings in the present life come into existence by themselves, without causes and conditions. As this view rejects all causality it is known as the "completely base opinion" (*sabbahīna-vāda*).

But the Buddha, on this occasion speaking to a young brahmin, desired to refute the creation rooted in God view and the no cause no condition view; so he declared, "Beings are the owners of their kamma, young man, the heirs to their kammas…."

He declared this in a general way. He did *not* say: "Beings are the owners of their *past* kamma, the heirs to their *past* kamma." In a passage addressed to the young brahmin, Subha, the words "owners of their kamma" and "heirs to their kamma" refer to both past life and present-life kamma. So one should understand this passage in this way: "Beings are the owners of their past and present kammas."

2. *The heirs to their kamma*

Only the wholesome and unwholesome deeds done by all beings are their inherited properties that always accompany them wherever they may wander in many lives and world cycles. Those who inherit from their parents are called their heirs, but they are not so in the true sense of this word. Why is this? Because things like gold, silver, jewels, and wealth only last temporarily, and those who inherit such temporary things cannot be called true and real heirs. Such legacies are our property only until death and when we die we have to leave it all behind. Certainly it does not accompany us into the future life. Also, legacies like this are subject to destruction by fire, water, thieves, and so on, before our death takes place, or they may be used up by us during our lives.

When we consider the three kinds of kamma, however, they belong to the beings who made them, even through future lives. They can never be destroyed by other persons or exterior forces, and for this reason kamma is said to be the only property inherited by beings. Beings are sure to reap the results of their own kamma in succeeding existences. Even feeding animals such as pigs, dogs, and birds can result in many births full of happiness, while the wholesome kamma made by offering food to virtuous bhikkhus (monks) can give rise to countless numbers of happy lives as man or deva. From the gift of almsfood worth half a crown in this life may come beneficial results worth thousands of pounds in future existences.[11] And if a person kills an animal, such as a fish, fowl, or pig, he may in turn have to suffer being killed in more than a thousand future lives.

---

11 The text is worded in terms of Burmese currency.

This may be illustrated by the banyan tree, for if one of its tiny seeds is planted, a great tree will grow out of it, bearing innumerable fruits during a thousand years or more. The same will be true of mango or jak seeds from which will grow large trees yielding thousands of fruits in the course of many, many years.

Just as a small seed is able to yield thousands of fruits, leaves, branches, and twigs, so a seed of wholesome kamma such as almsgiving, moral conduct, and meditation can bear in future lives good results many thousands of times over. Likewise, an unwholesome kamma-seed, such as destroying a living being, can yield evil and painful results in numerous future existences.

From just one kamma made by some person the results will follow him in many lives as pleasure or pain, when conditions are opportune. He can never be rid of that past kamma (until its force is exhausted, its fruits ripened completely), but has to enjoy or suffer its results. For this reason the Buddha has declared: "*All beings are the heirs to their kammas.*"

Look at it another way.[12] A being has two groups (*khandhas*)—the body-group and the mind-group (*rūpakkhandha, nāmakkhandha*). The first means the body with head, hands, legs, and so on, while the mind-group refers to thoughts and consciousness.

Of these two, the body-group comes to dissolution once in each existence, in each life having different shape and color (according to kamma, parental appearance, etc.). But the mind has no break in its continuity, and mental states arise and pass away successively through innumerable existences. Wholesome kamma, such as

---

12 This passage forms an Appendix in the English booklet, but has been added here.

giving and moral conduct, causes the subsequent arising in happy existences. And wherever the mind-group arises there a new and appropriate body-group is formed. In the same way, unwholesome kamma brings about the arising of mind in the lower states of existence, such as among dogs, pigs, fowl, and birds, where a body will be formed according to that arising. So a person is also "heir to kamma" with regard to these two groups.

3. Born of their kamma

Only the wholesome and unwholesome deeds done by beings are the origin of their wanderings in so many life cycles. To illustrate this, let us take the example of the banyan tree again. For its growth there are several causes: the banyan seed is the primary cause; the earth and water are secondary causes.

Wholesome past deeds such as almsgiving, moral conduct, etc., which cause one to be reborn as a human being, and the past unwholesome deeds such as destroying life, etc., causing one to be reborn as an animal, are the primary causes, comparable to the banyan seed. One's parents are the secondary causes, just as earth and water are secondary causes for the growth of the banyan tree.

To take another example: working as a laborer for wages, the present kamma is the primary cause, while the place of work, spade, basket, and the employers who pay the wages are the secondary cause. In the same way, one's own kamma made in the present existence with wisdom or without it is the primary cause; present results, pleasant and painful, are the wages for these actions.

So we can see that both past kamma and the kamma made in this life are primary causes of the results experienced, and one's parents are not primary causes. Nor has it anything to do with a God. And so the Buddha declares: *"All beings are born of their kamma."*

4. Related to their kamma

Only the wholesome and unwholesome kammas made by beings are their relatives and true friends (or false friends in the case of unwholesome kammas!), always accompanying them wherever they may wander through many lives and world cycles.

By way of explanation we can say that although there are parents, brothers, children, relatives, teachers, and friends whom we love and rely upon, we can only do this for a short time—until our death. But one's own physical, verbal, and mental deeds are constant companions who accompany one and give happiness and prosperity (or misery) in one's future lives. So wholesome deeds alone are one's true relatives and friends who should be esteemed and relied upon. Therefore the Buddha declares: *"All beings are related to their kamma."*

5. Abide supported by their kamma[13]

Only the wholesome and unwholesome deeds done by beings are their real support wherever they may wander through many lives and world cycles.

---

13 This phrase is *kamma-paṭisaraṇa* in Pāli. *Saraṇa* has the meaning of refuge, as in the Three Refuges (*tisaraṇa*), but to use this as the original translator has done is awkward since it makes no sense to talk of past unwholesome kamma as a refuge, though it can be one's support. There is some ambivalence of explanation of this factor.

To explain this: the word "support" means what can be relied upon, or what one can take shelter in, what can save or give protection against troubles and dangers. Those who wish to enjoy long life in the world have to rely upon food and drink as the protection against the danger of starvation. Similarly, doctors and medicine are needed for protection against bodily troubles and diseases, while weapons are protection against enemies. (And all kinds of support or refuge in the world may be considered in the same way.) So this word '*saraṇa*' does not refer only to the Going for Refuge at a shrine or in the presence of a bhikkhu, it means also reliance upon and taking shelter, as was explained already.

Now how is kamma one's support? In this life an ordinary man with no possessions soon comes to distress. Fearing to experience this we are supported by the work (or kamma) which we do and so acquire money and possessions.

Again, as a lack of wholesome kamma leads to rebirth in the lower worlds where there is grievous suffering, so fearful of this, some people make wholesome kamma leading them to rebirth as human beings or as devas.

Just as the present kamma made by work using knowledge and wisdom can protect us from dangers in this life, in the same way wholesome kamma such as almsgiving and moral conduct protects us from the dangers of future lives in the lower worlds. As we must rely on our work in this life, so we must also rely on wholesome kamma for the future. It is for this reason that the Buddha declares: "*All beings are supported by their kamma.*"

This subject of support or refuge should be analyzed as follows.

In the Buddhist religion there are four refuges for the future: (1) the Buddha, (2) the Dhamma, (3) the Sangha, and (4) one's own wholesome kamma.

This can be compared to the four kinds of refuge or support for sick people. First is the chief physician, second the suitable medicine, third the assistant doctors, and fourth, the actions of the patient following their directions confidently. In this simile, the chief physician and the assistant doctors are accounted as supports (or refuges) for the patient because they are capable of prescribing suitable medicines for this particular ailment, while the medicine is his support in that it can actually cure him. The sensible actions of the patient in following the doctor's directions are also his support, for without such actions on his part the other three supports would be ineffective and he could not be cured. All four can be clearly seen to be real supports or refuges for sick people.

Now persons who make evil kamma and indulge in sensual pleasures are like those sick people. The Buddha is like the chief physician, an expert in curing afflictions. The assistant doctors represent the Order of Bhikkhus, while the Dhamma is pictured as the medicine. The bodily, verbal, and mental wholesome deeds are like those sensible actions of the ailing man in which he follows the doctor's instructions.

In this way we can reckon that there are four refuges (or supports) in the Buddha's Teaching, and of these four, three—the Buddha, Dhamma, and Sangha—are not found outside (in other teachings). The fourth refuge or support, making wholesome kamma, exists both within and outside Buddhism. While we are commoners (*puthujjana*) we shall never be free of making kamma and experiencing results of kamma—for kamma and its fruits are in operation for all beings in the world system—so it is wise to make only wholesome kamma.

So we see that the subject of "All beings are owners of their kamma" applies to all beings in all world systems, whether Buddhism exists there or not. It is for this reason that the support (or refuge) in kamma has been dealt with here but not the Three Refuges of Buddhists. Together these form four refuges or supports that can be relied upon both for good and wise conduct in this life and for rebirth in the happy existences.

We have noted already that *saraṇa,* usually translated "refuge," means that which can save, give support or protection, so that food and drink are the *support* for long life, medicines and diet are the *support* for the sick, kings and rulers are *protection* against bandits and thieves, buildings are *protection* against the elements and for comfortable living, boats are a *support* for those who travel on water. Similarly, the earth is a *support,* and so are water, fire, and air for their respective purposes. So there are numerous supports or refuges in this existence. This concludes the exposition about the different kinds of refuges in Buddhism.

Refuge in other religions

Religions apart from Buddhism have only one refuge—that is, refuge in God. Whatever comes into existence and whatever is destroyed is therefore attributed to God.

I shall clarify this point. In religions such as Christianity and Islam[14] the bare meaning of refuge—in

---

14 The venerable author's treatment of this point applies to Hinduism only in part since there is here generally a belief in kamma and in one or more gods who have some or all of the attributes of the Biblical God as Creator, Judge, Compassionate Father, etc. When kamma and such god-belief are brought together

making good kamma—is not understood so that followers regard God as their only refuge. They assume that the appearance and disappearance of the world and of the beings on it is due to the power of God. So they believe that God saves those who have faith in him by means of his supernormal power. And by means of this power he can wash away all the sins and evils done by beings, giving them eternal happiness and eternal life after death. Thus the good and bad things experienced by beings depend on the will of God.

People like this disbelieve in kamma and do not think that it can be the cause of results. It is really very surprising that people who are making kamma all the time, in this way disregard their own actions.[15] Kamma, as we have already said, means all intentional physical, verbal, and mental actions. Now all of these actions are done by people, whether Buddhist or otherwise, and some will be done by non-Buddhists in the worship of their religions, whatever forms it takes. So they make kamma by practicing and undertaking such things as baptism, worship of God with body, speech and mind, obedience to his commandments, prostrations and offerings; all these things, as they are intentional, are kamma. Though these outsiders believe that God saves those who have faith in him and perform such actions (and does not save those who do not know of him or believe in him and who therefore do not do these things), really there is just the kamma made by those people who in time will receive its fruits, from their own hearts, not from God.

---

there is confusion, as it is not clear whether what one experiences is to be attributed to one's kamma or to God.

15 For if one understands clearly the law of kamma and its fruits there is no room for the God-idea.

In these God-worshipping religions, as in Buddhism, one can also discern four refuges (supports), even though only one is usually spoken of. They are:

(1) God;
(2) the commandments and teachings of God;
(3) prophets such as Mohammed or saviours such as Christ, and the saints and priesthood; and
(4) the kamma made in the performance of religious rites and duties.

The priests and missionaries of those religions do not realize that even in their own teachings there are several kinds of refuge. They do not analyze but treat God as their only refuge, disregarding kamma. Thus they believe in something which is in some senses "outside" and different from themselves, rather than kamma which is "inside" (one's own mind, speech, and body) and certainly part of oneself. Consequently they believe that the good and evil, prosperity and poverty, happiness and suffering of all beings, are created only by God and not due to other causes. They do not know that there are various and different causes for these events.

Is it simply by worship, by praying to God, that poor people who deserve wealth can obtain it? Would they not get it rather by their present kamma while diligently working as a laborer, farmer, or trader? (Note that "kamma" can mean labor or work as well as morally productive action.)

The answer to these questions which accords with cause and effect is that wealth is not usually obtained by prayer to God, whereas acquisition of property is clearly evident as a result of present kamma. As such is the case, it is believable that wealth in this life is got by making kamma now, and has nothing to do with God.

God has no power to give things to people, but present kamma can do so.[16] If God had such power then his followers would have no need to work (i.e. to make present kamma), for they would all enjoy riches given by him. Also those who do not believe in him would not get anything even though they worked (i.e. made kamma) diligently. But this is not so. Devout followers of a God have to work and make kamma in order to obtain wealth, while those who are not his followers can also become rich by making the appropriate kamma. We do not find only wealthy God-believers; on the contrary there are many poor people among them. Therefore, consideration of these reasons shows that acquisition of wealth in this life is the result of present kamma. It is not a gift of God.

In the same way, if one desires education and knowledge, it can be obtained by the present kamma of studying and learning. But it cannot be got by the worship of God.

Again, if one wishes to become a government officer, it is necessary to study the requirements for particular posts. Government jobs cannot be obtained by praying to God.

So we can see for ourselves that all worldly gains are obtainable only by the power of present kamma, not by the supposed power of God.

Let us examine another side to this matter. God-believers have faith that by humbly worshipping God

---

16 Many of the "prayers answered by God" and "miracle cures" are due to present kamma. Example: devotee enters a church, mosque, or temple and prays. The mind becomes calm—peace and happiness results—an answer is born in the calm mind which could not arise because of grief in the agitated mind. The prayer is "answered" or the "cure" effected by the intense faith of the sufferer. No God is needed.

they are freed from their sins and evils, including sickness. However, generally the sick are not cured only by taking the refuge and support of God; for a cure most of them must treat their bodies with medicines and diets. It is the present kamma made by regulating the body in this way that is the cause of their cure. Everyone has seen this for themselves, for Buddhists who are not believers in God and the God-believers all can be cured if the right conditions are present.

How surprising it is that God-believers think that they can be freed in the next life from the results of their sins in this one just by worshipping God sincerely, when even a disease such as ringworm in this life cannot be cured in this way!

It is surprising, too, that as even trifling wealth cannot be got in this life by praying to God, they believe the wealth of everlasting life and happiness in heaven can be acquired in this way!

Now since we have seen for ourselves that wealth and happiness not yet attained in this life are got by virtue of the different ways of making good kamma, not by the favor of God, we can fully believe that there is no other refuge apart from present kamma to get these things.

In the same way, we can believe that attainments of some higher plane of existence, a heaven world (*devaloka*), after death, is also due to present kamma. This has nothing to do with God, for a person who has made no wholesome kamma cannot be reborn in a higher plane by the fiat of God, while those who do not believe in him or worship him but have made wholesome kamma can certainly attain to higher states of existence.[17]

---

17 This paragraph is from the *Sammādiṭṭhi-dīpanī*.

As to what is called "eternal salvation," those who believe in God, take refuge in him, and revere him throughout their lives believe that only such persons as themselves, believing as they do, can be saved by him when they die, while non-believers will not be saved. But it is quite clear that such believers are not saved by God at all but by their own kamma of "believing in God," "taking refuge in God," and "revering God." God is thus a concept, a conditioned phenomenon, in the minds of such believers.

The various beneficial results in a future life of present wholesome kamma cover such possibilities as rebirth into a ruling family or one that is prosperous, and rebirth in the deva-worlds or the Brahma-worlds as a deva or Brahmā.[18]

Knowing the power of kamma the Buddha has declared: *"All beings abide supported by their kammas."*

6. *Whatever kamma they shall do, whether good or evil, of that they will be the heirs*

When bodily, verbal, and mental kammas have been made, whether wholesome or unwholesome, the beings who have individually made them will receive their fruits even after many lives or aeons.

---

18 A deva is a being with a subtle body and superlative sense pleasures. He may be, at lowest, a local spirit of a tree, river, rock and so on, or at highest an inhabitant of the plane of "deities wielding power over others' creations" (*paranimmita-vasavatti deva*). For such birth some purification of mind is needed but no great success in meditation. But for birth in the Brahma-worlds it is necessary to attain jhāna, intense inward concentration, as a result of which there is a partial purification of mind. The Brahma-worlds are more tranquil and less sensual than the deva-worlds.

(The first five phrases of the quotation which have been used as headings above refer to past kamma which bears fruit in the present life, but this sixth phrase concerns present kamma which will bear fruit in the future.)

The explanation of the right view on the ownership of one's kamma is finished.

* * *

B. Right View regarding the Ten Subjects

This means having right view of the following ten matters. The Buddha has said:

> "There is (moral significance in) giving alms. There is (moral significance in) large offerings. There is (moral significance in) small gifts. There is the result and fruit of good and bad deeds. There is (moral significance in what is done to) one's mother. There is (moral significance in what is done to) one's father. There are beings of instantaneous rebirth. There is this world, there is another world. There are in the world ascetics and brahmins of right attainment, of right practice who, having realized by their own super-knowledge (the truth regarding) this world and other worlds, make it known to others."

By way of explanation we can say:

1. There is (moral significance in) almsgiving[19]

This is the right view that almsgiving—such as giving food to animals, to lay people, to bhikkhus, and so on—if done with benevolence, leads to beneficial results, that kamma in a previous existence sometimes bears fruit in subsequent existences.

2. There is (moral significance in) large offerings

The right view that generosity, performed with faith and respect for the virtuous qualities of the recipient, yields beneficial results in the future.

3. There is (moral significance in) small gifts

The right view that gifts, even those given on a small scale, if given with loving kindness, bring benefit to the doer in the future.

4. There is the result and fruit of good and bad deeds

The right view that cruel actions done in previous lives yield painful results in future lives, while refraining from such evil deeds and cultivating wholesome deeds subsequently bears the fruit of happiness.

---

19 The Pāli has only the rather terse "There is almsgiving" but the Buddha's intention in making such a statement was to refute those non-Buddhist teachers in his time who taught that neither good kamma nor bad kamma bear any results. See Makkhali Gosāla in *Dictionary of Pāli Proper Names*.

5–6. There is (moral significance in what is done to) one's mother and to one's father[20]

The right view that good and evil deeds done towards one's mother or father bear pleasant and painful fruits respectively, possibly in future lives.

7. There are beings of instantaneous rebirth

The right view that there really are beings born instantaneously who are (generally) invisible to human eyes. Instantaneous rebirth refers to those beings who do not take conception in a womb. Due to the force of their previous kamma they are born complete with limbs and other organs of the body which need no development further but remain as they are.

Mahābrahmā, the being of greatest power in this world system, has his abode in the three lowest planes of the Brahma-world. He is regarded as God in other religions in which the existence of still higher planes is usually unknown.[21]

Even when men are close to such beings, they are generally unable to see them with human eyes. Only when those beings cause their forms to become visible can they be seen by people here. Normally they are

---

20 Mother and father, especially in their old age, should be treated well by their children—out of gratitude and love for what they have done for oneself. The fruits of maltreatment of parents will be long and painful. Their hard work for their children can only be repaid by teaching them the Dhamma. (see *Anguttara Nikāya* I, pp.11–12).

21 For this see the Discourse on the Invitation of Brahmā (*Majjhima Nikāya* 49), *Middle Length Sayings* I, pp.388ff. See also *Buddhism and the God-Idea*, Wheel No. 47.

invisible to human beings[22] just like God, the angels, and devils of other religions.

The understanding that there really are such beings born instantaneously is also called right view.

8. There is this world

The right view of this world as the human world (one of several planes in the level of sensuality and lowest among the planes of good rebirth).

9. There is another world[23]

The right view that "another world" (i.e. states of existence differing from this one) consisting of the four planes of lower birth—hells, animals, ghosts, and titans, collectively known as the planes of deprivation—together with the devā and the Brahma-planes, really do exist.

In other religions, apart from the human and animal planes, these worlds are not known properly. (The heaven-worlds of the devas and the hell-worlds may be thought of as permanent when they are really impermanent states of long existence; the ghosts and titans may be ignored except in exorcism rites, while even the animals are not understood properly as beings also in the round of birth and death.)[24]

---

22 Human eyes can perceive only a small range of the light radiations, similarly with human ears. A large range of waves cannot be perceived through human senses so that much of the world system remains unknown unless explored by way of the mind.

23 Those people who say "I am a Buddhist but I don't believe in other states of rebirth"—please note!

24 See *The Wheel of Birth and Death*, Wheel No. 147/149.

Another explanation is possible of the last two phrases: that this world system with its human world, the four lower worlds, the heavenly deva and Brahma-worlds, are termed "this world," while in all directions from this world system there are an infinite number of other world systems which are called "the other world(s)." These world systems are generally not recognized in other religions.[25]

10. There are in the world ascetics and brahmins of right attainment, of right practice, who having realized by their own super-knowledge (the truth regarding) this world and other worlds, make it known to others

There are such possibilities for spiritual development as the super-knowledges (*abhiññā*),[26] and the all-knowing knowledge (*sabbaññuta-ñaṇa*).[27] Ascetics and brahmins who exert themselves diligently in performing the perfections (*pāramī*) and practicing the meditations through calm and insight in this very world can attain

---

25 Note in this respect recent Christian concern as to whether Christ's message will save beings on other planets. Buddhism has always known of an infinity of inhabited worlds where the Four Noble Truths must always be true.

26 Super-knowledges are five or six in number as generally listed: the magical powers, the divine eye (clairvoyance—the venerable author refers to this super-knowledge below), the divine ear (clairaudience), knowledge of past lives, knowledge of kamma and its results. These five can be experienced by non-Buddhists also, but the sixth, the destruction of the pollutions (*āsavakkhaya*), is only won by those who develop path and fruit wisdom (*magga-phala-ñāṇa*), difficult to find outside Buddhism.

27 Note that the Buddha disclaimed that he was omniscient in the sense that he knew everything at the same time. But he said it was possible for him to know everything about a particular subject if he turned his mind to it.

such knowledges. Such people are born into this world from time to time who, because of their efforts and practice in past lives, are possessed of these knowledges.

But some people, due to their limited *pāramī* or perfections, are only able to gain the super-knowledges, and then they can see the four lower worlds, the six deva-worlds and some of the Brahma-worlds, just as if they looked at them with their usual human eyes. Other people are capable of both the super-knowledges and the all-knowing knowledge so that they see clearly all the countless beings, the infinite worlds and world systems. People who have both these knowledges are called "Buddhas."

These two kinds of people appear in the human world from time to time and impart their knowledge of this world and other worlds to others who often become their followers. But it is only a Buddha who can explain the round of rebirth in terms of cause and effect and clarify the arising and passing away even of the world systems.

In regard to this there are three kinds of understanding (1) that beings with super-knowledges and the all-knowing knowledge do appear in this world from time to time; (2) that their teaching if based on the six super-knowledges is thoroughly reliable, and if on five of them at least partly so; (3) that other worlds do exist. All this constitutes right view.

Those who have this right view do not doubt that a Buddha arises only in the human world, not in the heavenly worlds. But in religions where such right view is not understood they imagine that the all-knowers and all-seers, those having the all-knowing knowledge, appear only in the highest heavens and not in the human world. Only in the human world can one strive towards the all-knowing knowledge. Why is this so? The devas and Brahmās are too comfortable—they see no suffering, their lives are too long so they do not see impermanence. But the beings in the planes of deprivation have so much suffering that they cannot practice Dhamma. Only human beings have rather short lives and so are pricked by impermanence, only they have a mixture of pleasure and pain. Diligent effort is needed if one would attain the all-knowing knowledge and those who are able to make this effort are human beings. And it is the rare human being who attains Buddhahood here in this human world. This is the marvel and the wonder of a Buddha, that he is a human being, not a deva or Brahmā. If he were such a heavenly inhabitant then there would be nothing very remarkable about his knowledge and wisdom. But as he is born normally of human parents and has a body essentially the same as that of all other people, he is wonderful and marvellous for showing what a human being can attain to if he makes the effort.

It is only in the Buddha's Dhamma that profound, sublime, and wonderful teachings are found, for they are revealed by the Buddha's all-knowing knowledge. They all belong to the sphere of super-knowledge, hard to find outside Buddhism.

One should know that there are two spheres of power: the power of knowledge and the power of kamma. In the latter, the most effective is the power of jhāna (intense concentration) which is a "heavy" kamma. It can cause one to arise in the form or formless planes as a Brahmā with an immensely long span of life. But the power of kamma cannot cause one to become a Perfectly Enlightened One. Even though one has made the merits to be reborn as Mahābrahmā himself, still one has no super-knowledge to know and see all.

To strive in this life to become a wealthy person is one path, while to strive for insight knowledge and so become a teacher for other beings is another. Striving to become a Mahābrahmā is similar to the effort to attain wealth, while to strive as a bhikkhu or lay hermit for insight knowledge is actually the way of the Buddha and the arahants.

Here is another example. Birds such as parrots, crows, and vultures have wings with which to fly but they do not possess knowledge and wisdom like men. Human beings have varying degrees of knowledge and wisdom but having no wings they are unable by themselves to fly.

The wholesome kammas which the Mahābrahmās have made by developing jhāna, and the wholesome kammas of the devas residing both here on earth and in the various deva-worlds, resemble the wings of birds. But the super-knowledges and the all-knowing knowledge of lay hermits and bhikkhus are like the wisdom of the man in the above example.

It is due to the power of their wholesome kamma made by developing jhāna that the Mahābrahmās live in the higher planes of existence, long-lived and powerful. But they do not possess the two kinds of super-knowledge and so do not penetrate the deep truths of impermanence, suffering, non-self, and voidness. Their knowledge is confined to just what they experience personally.

To summarize some important points of this section, we can note that the knowledge which makes clear: (1) that a Buddha has the all-knowing knowledge and arises only in the human plane, not in the higher planes of existence; (2) that only ascetics of the human race complete in the super-knowledges and in the all-knowing knowledge can clearly teach the conditioned

THE PLANES OF EXISTANCE

4 FORMLESS ATTAINMENTS	o	The Base consisting of neither-perception-nor-non-perception (the Summit of Existence)	20 PLANES OF THE BRAHMA — WORLD	FORMLESS REALM	THE GOOD DESTINATIONS
	o	The Base consisting of nothingness			
	o	The Base consisting of infinity of consciousness			
	o	The Base consisting of infinity of space			
		FORM DISAPPEARS			
PURE ABODES OF NON-RETURNERS	o	Akaniṭṭha (junior to none)		(SUBTLE) FORM REALM	
	o	Sudassī (fair-seeing)			
	o	Sudassa (fair-to-see)			
	o	Ātappa (untormenting)			
	o	Aviha (bathed in their own prosperity)			
4th JHANA	o	Asaññasatta (non-percipient beings)			
	o	Vehapphala (very fruitful)			
3rd JHANA	o	Subhakiṇṇa (refulgent glory)			
	o	Appamāṇasubha (measureless glory)			
	o	Parittasubha (limited glory)			
2nd JHANA	o	Ābhassara (streaming radiance)			
	o	Appamāṇābha (measureless radtance)			
	o	Parittābha (limited radiance)			
1st JHANA	o	Mahābrahma (Great Brahmā)			
	o	Brahmapurohita (Brahma's Ministers)			
	o	Brahmapārisajja (Brahma's retinue)			

<table>
<tr><td></td><td></td><td>FIVE HINDRANCES DISAPPEAR</td><td></td><td></td><td></td></tr>
<tr><td rowspan="6">FAITH GENERO–SITY AND 8 PRECEPTS</td><td>O</td><td>Paranimmitavasavattī (wielding power over others' creations</td><td rowspan="6">SENSUALITY REALM HEAVENS</td><td rowspan="11">SENSUALITY REALM</td><td rowspan="7"></td></tr>
<tr><td>O</td><td>Nimmānarati (delight in creating)</td></tr>
<tr><td>O</td><td>Tusita (contented)</td></tr>
<tr><td>O</td><td>Yāma (gone to bliss)</td></tr>
<tr><td>O</td><td>Tāvatiṃsa (thirty-three)</td></tr>
<tr><td>O</td><td>Cātumaharājika (four great kings)</td></tr>
<tr><td>5 PRECEPTS</td><td>Womb born</td><td colspan="2">Human beings (manussa)</td></tr>
<tr><td>DESIRE FOR POWER</td><td>O</td><td colspan="2">Demons (asura)</td><td rowspan="4">THE BAD DESTINATIONS OR STATES OF DEPRIVATION</td></tr>
<tr><td>MEANNESS, ATTACHMENT</td><td>O</td><td colspan="2">Ghosts (peta)</td></tr>
<tr><td>STUPIDITY, ANIMAL DESIRES</td><td>Womb born
Egg born</td><td colspan="2">Animals (tiracchāna)</td></tr>
<tr><td>CRUELTY, TORTURE, KILLING</td><td>O</td><td colspan="2">beings in Hell = the World of Yama, or Niraya.</td></tr>
</table>

O = *Opapayika* = *Instantaneous Rebirth*

nature of aeons and world systems, how beings wander in the round of birth and death and how wholesome and unwholesome kamma operates; and (3) that the teachings of the monks compiled as the Sutta (Discourses), Vinaya (Discipline), and Abhidhamma are true, is called the *right-view knowledge that there are (enlightened) ascetics and brahmins in the world*.

On the other hand, wrong views should be rejected, such as the view that an Enlightened One with the all-knowing knowledge does not appear in the human plane but only in the highest heavenly abode. Also that the gods are not many but only one God, as well as the idea that this one God, being highest and noblest, must be eternal and free from decay, disease, and death.

The Buddha has rejected all such tangles of views.

C. Right View of the Four Noble Truths

This right view means:

(1) Knowledge of real suffering.
(2) Knowledge of the true causal arising of suffering.
(3) Knowledge of the cessation of suffering.
(4) Knowledge of that right path leading to the cessation of suffering.[28]

---

28 The following explanation of the Four Noble Truths is brief. For a detailed explanation see the author's *Explanation of the Four Truths* (*Catusacca-dīpanī*) translated in *The Light of the Dhamma*, Vol. V, No. 4 and Vol. VI, No. 1, 1958–59).

1. *Right View of the Truth of Suffering*

Attachment to sensuality and the troubles caused thereby

Because of this attachment, human beings, devas, and Brahmās are subject to great pains and sufferings which have existed in the past, continue in the present, and will be experienced, while attachment remains, in the future. The eye, ear, nose, tongue, body (touch), and mind are the six internal sense-spheres which operate, in the unenlightened person, in conjunction with defilements of greed, aversion, and delusion whenever they are stimulated by an external sense object. These six sense faculties are the suffering which, though not apparent to many people, is real, constant, and oppressive.

How does attachment to the senses oppress? It may be explained by this group of factors: kamma-formations, instability, and suffering. In another way there is oppression through kamma-formations, burning, and instability. Or it can be explained through birth, decay, and death. Again, there is oppression by way of stoking up the fires of greed, aversion, and delusion, conceit, wrong view, the mental defilements (*kilesa*) and the pollutions (*āsava*), by stimulating evil conduct such as destroying living creatures and so on, or by fuelling the fires of birth, decay, sorrow, lamentation, pain, grief, and despair.

Now I shall explain some of these points.

Oppression by kamma-formations (saṇkhārā)

Possession of the sense faculties of a human being, deva, or Brahmā means that good kamma has been made in a past life, for if good kamma had not been made the senses of a hell-being, animal, ghost, or titan would have come into existence. So the senses of a higher being are oppressive to him because of the good kamma-formations which must be made continually to ensure the continuation of those faculties. And those same kamma-formations oppress him in the next existence also because he has still to protect and sustain his conduct so that he will not lose those sense faculties in the future. So there comes about a constant oppression. As the eye and other senses do not arise independently of the kamma-formations, it is said that kamma-formations always "oppress" the "owner" of those senses throughout the beginningless round of birth and death.

Oppression by instability (vipariṇāma)

This means "oppression by liability to immediate destruction, whenever cause exists for destruction." From the time of conception onwards there is not a single moment, even for the winking of an eye or a flash of lightning, when there is no liability to destruction. Moreover, there is always the anxiety caused by impending destruction. And when destruction comes, then many sorts of suffering have to be experienced. This is what is meant by saying that the senses are oppressive because of their instability.

Oppression by the painfulness of suffering

This means both physical and mental suffering. The suffering experienced while the sense bases grow (in the womb) and the experience by way of them during birth needs no comment. The painfulness of suffering is also evident when the senses come into contact with an unpleasant object. Also, whenever one inflicts bodily pain upon others out of the unpleasant feelings which arise when seeing or hearing them—then this oppression is experienced. And when the eye or another sense organ contracts some disease, or whenever there is physical and mental trouble in the preservation and protection of the eye, etc., then oppression by suffering occurs. In this way all the senses beginning with the eye oppress beings with the suffering associated with them.

Oppression by burning (santāpa)

The senses are the source of so much suffering by means of the defilements which they awaken in the hearts of people. These defilements are like great fires which are continually refuelled and burn without dying down from the beginningless past to the endless future in the round of birth and death. These great fires are three in number: the fires of greed, aversion, and delusion, and when they are refuelled through the eye, ear, nose, tongue, body, and mind, they ensure that one's future in saṃsāra will be long and miserable.

It is right-view knowledge that gives one understanding of the immense sea of sufferings born of attachment to sense pleasures, whether in the sensuality sphere, the fine-form sphere, or the formless sphere.

2. *Right View of the Causal Arising of Suffering*

In the round of birth and death, so long as there is attachment to the senses as "mine" or "myself," so long continues oppressiveness and suffering. So it is craving, desire, and greed connected with the senses that is the true cause for the arising of suffering.[29]

---

29 One should not understand craving as the one and only cause. Where craving (*taṇhā*) is found, there will be ignorance (of the Four Noble Truths) as well as other factors of dependent origination.

It is right-view knowledge that gives one understanding of the causal arising of suffering by way of craving.

3. Right View of the Cessation of Suffering

In whatever life the craving and greed connected with the senses finally cease, the suffering and oppression finally cease as well. The senses do not arise again after the death of the person who has extinguished craving.

It is right-view knowledge that gives one understanding of the cessation of craving.

4. Right View of the Path Leading to the Cessation of Suffering

When, as a result of practicing Dhamma in general and developing the mind in meditation in particular, the true nature of the senses is seen and understood, craving connected with them ceases in this very life. It does not arise again and so sense oppression likewise does not arise.

It is right-view knowledge that gives one understanding of the true path leading to the cessation of craving. Among all the parts of the Noble Eightfold Path, this right view of the Four Noble Truths is most essential.

This concludes the brief exposition of right view of the Four Truths.

II. Right Thought[30]

This is explained under three headings:

1. Thoughts of renunciation (i.e. generosity).
2. Thoughts of non-harming (i.e. loving kindness).
3. Thoughts of non-violence (i.e. compassion).[31]

1. Thoughts of Renunciation

The mental state where there is absence of greed and ability therefore to renounce the five sense pleasures, that is pleasant sights, sounds, smells, tastes, and touches. Or it is ability to renounce attachment to the five groups (*khandha*), or to mind and body. Thought arising out of such absence of greed is this mode of right thought.[32]

---

30 *Saṅkappa*, a word not easy to translate. The translation "thought" does not convey the emotional connotation of the three kinds of *saṅkappa*. "Intention" is sometimes used.

31 These three terms seem to have been chosen by the Buddha for their wide range of possible meanings. The negative terms for positive mental states (common usage in Pāli) makes for a range of possible meanings which a positive term would not be able to express.

32 Here is a place where giving comes into the path; we have already seen it mentioned under right view. "Renunciation" does not necessarily imply cutting off one's hair and leading a homeless life; here the emphasis is on interior renunciation. If one is able, to start with, to loosen one's greed and attachment to things, it is possible then to become generous in giving to others. This is the first step, in one sense, along any spiritual path. For if material possessions cannot be given up for the benefit of other living beings, what hope is there of progressing further along that path where greater renunciation, as explained by the author, must be made? The renunciation spoken of here is not something forced, though one

2. Thoughts of Non-Harming

Loving kindness (*mettā*) for all beings, visible such as men and animals, or invisible such as devas and ghosts; the mind or heart which wishes their good and welfare.[33]

3. Thoughts of Non-Violence

Compassion and sympathy for all beings, all of whom are subject to some suffering while most beings have much suffering to bear. Thoughts which, to use the Pāli idiom, "tremble with" the sufferings of others are the practice of this aspect of right thought.[34]

This finishes the explanation of right thought.

---

should make efforts to be more generous. It comes quite naturally with the practice of the other path factors. When right concentration is practiced and some success in it attained then the things of this world become less interesting and can be given away or given up quite naturally and easily. Generous giving and giving up must be cultivated for successful practice of the Buddha's Dhamma. Without it, though one may have much knowledge, all one's Dhamma stays in the head, or comes out of the mouth—it is never expressed through the hands. No one can be a successful cultivator of the path unless they support liberally the Buddha, Dhamma, and Sangha, and are generous to other people in general.

33 This is a very short notice of a most important subject! A person can claim to be a Buddhist and certainly have right view as defined in the previous section but still have enmity towards others or speak slander about them. All one's book learning will not change harmfulness into loving kindness; only Dhamma practice, particularly the development of *mettā* through meditation, can do this. This means hard work on oneself which may be painful emotionally but then the result of accomplishing just a little here is that one becomes a "solid" Buddhist, not just one with a Buddhist facade. And, of course, one gains many good friends.

34 The meditative aspect of loving kindness and compassion has been emphasized in these two sections as they constitute right

III. Right Speech

There are four types of right speech:

1. Restraint from false speech.
2. Restraint from tale-bearing.
3. Restraint from harsh talk.
4. Restraint from useless chatter.

The first of these means abstinence from both speaking untruth in such a way that it appears to be truth and speaking truth as though it were untruth.[35]

The second is found where a person abstains from bearing tales which would cause two friends to lose confidence and regard for each other, and so create dissension and trouble.

The third abstinence is from words uttered in anger which are rough, harsh, and abusive, such as insinuations regarding race, family, personality, and occupation.

And the fourth, abstinence from useless chatter, refers to such plays and novels[36] as contain no worthy

---

thought. This is implied by the practice of the first precept (see right action) and by the Buddha's constant exhortation to gentleness in dealing with others. One is not truly a Buddhist unless one's actions conform to Dhamma.

35 The first is common lying while the second refers to cunning ways of corrupting what is true so that it appears to be false.

36 "As *Enaung* and *Ngwedaung*" in the first English edition. Myanaung U Tin writes: "*Enaung* is a work of fiction written about 100 years ago during the reign of King Mindon. It is hardly known to the present generation. *Ngwedaung* is a legend relating to Kayah State on the borders of Thailand. It is still well known and often staged. Quite naturally, fiction, legend, and fairy tales are considered to be *samphappalāpa*." The reference is obviously to literature and drama which is liable to lead to deterioration, not to

goals (*attha*), no rightful means thereto (*dhamma*), and no reference to good conduct (*vinaya*). Such matters do not inspire those who read or listen to them though they may have transient entertainment value.

Words which relate to goals (a*ttha*) describe such things as long life, health, and rightly acquired wealth enjoyed in this life, while in a future life they are such good results as being born a human being or a deva.

Words relating to the means (*dhamma*) make clear the ways in which the above goals can be realized

Those words which deal with the rules of conduct (*vinaya*) for both laity and religious (the five, eight, ten, or 227 precepts) are the basis for the destruction of greed and aversion.

Now words about such goals, means, and good conduct are not found in the type of books and dramas referred to here, so narrating and acting works like this amounts to useless chatter.

Also included under this heading are the thirty-two types of vulgar talk[37] which are spiritually unbeneficial [and obstruct the noble fruits of stream-winning, etc., and also rebirth in the higher planes. They are as follows: talk about rulers, criminals, ministers of state, armies, dangers, battles, food, drink, clothing, dwellings, adornments, perfumes, relatives, vehicles, villages, towns, cities, provinces, women (or men), heroes, streets, baths, relations who have died, this and that, the origin of the world, the origin of the

---

growth in Dhamma.

37 "Vulgar (lit. animal-like) talk" is so called either because it is worthy only of animals—and if one sees the list of what is contained in it, most of it is what journalists call "news" (!)—or it is "animal talk" because it goes on all fours like animals and not in an upright way like human beings.

ocean, eternity views, annihilation views, worldly loss, worldly gain, self-indulgence, self-mortification].[38]

Anyone who wants to develop wisdom regarding goals, means, and good conduct should not waste time indulging in these thirty-two kinds of talk. Further, a person who is developing the meditation practices leading to calm (*samatha*) or to insight (*vipassanā*) should know the limits even of speech dealing with goals, means, and good conduct.

This ends the description of the four types of right speech.

IV. Right Action

This is threefold:

1. Restraint from killing living creatures.
2. Restraint from taking what is not given.
3. Restraint from wrong conduct in (sexual)[39] pleasures.

The first of these means the intentional killing or destroying of beings either by physical action or by verbal incitement ranging from killing the eggs of lice and bugs, or causing abortion, to the slaughter of living creatures including human beings.[40]

---

38 These brackets contain the material found in Appendix I in the first edition.

39 The pleasures (*kāmā*) mentioned under the third of the Five Precepts all relate to sex but here, as we shall see, other pleasures are included.

40 The kamma made in all these actions is unwholesome, but of course not all of the same strength. In dealing with the world

Restraint from taking what is not given means abstaining from taking, with intention to steal, living beings or non-living articles which have an owner, removing or appropriating them without the owner's consent either by physical effort or by inciting another to do so.

Restraint from wrong conduct in sexual pleasures means abstention from sex which will cause pain and suffering to others. Examples will be adultery (for this causes the disruption of marriage), rape, intercourse with minors protected by parents, etc., and the perversion of others. Included here also are abstention from the five kinds of intoxicants and gambling with cards, dice, and so on.[41]

This ends the explanation of three sorts of right action.

---

wisdom has to be used to decide what should and should not be done.

41 These three headings are the equivalent of the first three of the Five Precepts, each of which is prefaced by the phrases: "I undertake the rule of training to refrain from ..." Into the last of these three is incorporated the fifth precept on intoxicants, while the fourth has been explained already under right speech. Although the explanation of these precepts is brief, their importance cannot be too greatly emphasized. Unless they are practiced diligently there is no hope of developing the mind in meditation, or of gaining insight or wisdom.

On the lighter side, though serious enough when distortions of the Buddha's teachings are taught to others, is the following story. At a meeting of a Buddhist society, a lecturer was addressing people upon the Five Precepts. Coming to the last one, he commented that as the Buddha had taught the Middle Way, by this precept was meant neither drunkenness, which is one extreme, nor total abstention, the other extreme, but just drinking in moderation. The lecturer does not seem to have reflected that the same standards if applied to the other precepts will be astonishing indeed! Not wholesale murder, nor total abstention from killing,

V. Right Livelihood

1. Restraint from livelihood based on wrong conduct.
2. Restraint from livelihood based on improper means.
3. Restraint from livelihood based on deception of others.
4. Restraint from livelihood based on low worldly knowledges.

Wrong conduct means either the threefold unwholesome bodily action beginning with killing living creatures described under right action, or the fourfold unwholesome verbal action such as lying, described under right speech—any livelihood gained in this way will be wrong. So will be a living made by the sale of the five kinds of merchandise[42] which should not be sold. When one abstains from such wrong conduct in livelihood, right livelihood is practiced.

The second heading, improper means, refers to ways of wrong livelihood not to be practiced by the bhikkhus (Buddhist monks) and lay hermits (*isi*, the Pāli form of the Sanskrit word *rishi*, represented by a class of lay followers in Burma). These wrong ways of getting a

---

but just killing in moderation!

This is an illustration of how important it is to know the Buddha's explanations of each path factor, not one's own ideas however good they seem to be. It also illustrates how one's own views are colored by craving for pleasure, comfort, etc.

42 "Weapons, living beings, meat, intoxicants and poisons—these five kinds of merchandise should not be traded in" (*Aṅguttara Nikāya*, The Fives). This note is from the first edition. The words quoted are the Buddha's.

livelihood involve such matters as a bhikkhu giving flowers and fruit to families, or medical preparations, or flattering them in some way, or acting as their messenger. In such wrong ways, a bhikkhu may hope to increase his gains though actually he earns only contempt.

Under the third heading above, livelihood is gained by deceiving others and while much of this section applies to bhikkhus, it does have application to householders as well. Five sorts of deception are given, as follows. The first is all sorts of trickery so that people understand that one can work wonders or attain deep states of meditation or the noble paths and fruits, or feigning deportment so that they think one is an ariya (noble one), or again causing people to have a high opinion of oneself by pretending that one does not wish to receive alms and accepts only for the sake of the donors. The second is talk which pleases donors so that they make a gift, while the third is making all sorts of hints and gestures so that offerings are made. Fourth comes harassing a donor with words so that he is obliged to give in order to get rid of oneself, and fifth comes giving a small gift so as to get a bigger one. All this is trickery and deception.

The fourth heading, wrong livelihood based on low worldly knowledges, means that one gets a living by prognostication, by palmistry and interpreting other bodily marks, or by astrology and other such low arts which run contrary to the bhikkhu's practice of Dhamma. When bhikkhus and lay hermits refrain from such things their livelihood is pure in this respect.

This brings to an end the exposition of right livelihood.

VI. Right Effort

This path-factor is analyzed into four components. The first two deal with unwholesome volitional actions (kamma), divided into unwholesome mental states which have arisen and those which have not yet arisen. These two constantly cause anxiety, corruption, and debasement for living beings. The second two deal with wholesome kamma, either with those states which have arisen or those which have not. They always bring peace, purity, nobility, and progress for beings. Now to define these four in greater detail.

The ten paths of unwholesome kamma have already been mentioned. Now, whatever of those kammas have already arisen in the past or arise in the present, they are all called "arisen unwholesomeness." But if such kammas have not yet been made though one may be liable to make them in future, then this is called "unarisen unwholesomeness."

To illustrate wholesome kamma, arisen and unarisen, let us take the seven stages of purity:

Purity of moral conduct (attained by keeping precepts)
Purity of mind (attained by meditation)
Purity of view
Purity by overcoming doubt
Purity by knowledge and vision of what is and what is not the path
Purity by knowledge and vision of the practice-path
Purity by knowledge and vision (the last five attained by wisdom)

Now whatever purity has arisen in oneself in the past, or in the present, that is called "arisen wholesomeness." But the purities which one has not experienced, though one may do so in the future (provided that the necessary effort is made), are called "unarisen wholesomeness."

If the Noble Eightfold Path is practiced and developed in this life, then by virtue of its power the bad conduct already arisen will never arise again until one attains Nibbāna without remainder of grasping (when there is no possibility of its doing so). Also, by virtue of the Noble Eightfold Path the bad conduct which has not arisen in oneself during this life, but which could arise in future, will have no chance to arise at any time until Nibbāna without remainder of grasping is attained.

In the same way, when this path is practiced and developed here and now, due to its power any one of the purities which has already arisen for oneself becomes indestructible and constant until the attainment of Nibbāna without remainder of grasping. Likewise, the purities which so far have not arisen in oneself, which have not been attained or reached, by virtue of the Noble Eightfold Path are reached and attained in this life.

(In explaining the terms "arisen" and "unarisen" people can easily understand unwholesomeness by way of the ten evil paths of making kamma while wholesomeness can best be illustrated by the seven kinds of purification.)

Bhikkhus and lay people who have encountered the Buddha's teaching, being confident and faithful, should be convinced by these reasons that only right effort in the practice and development of the Noble Eightfold Path leads to their real welfare and prosperity. The things of this world should be carried out only in essential matters such as are unavoidable.

This is indeed the way of elucidating right effort which is a fundamental factor for Buddhist practice. The summary of this most important subject in relation to the Eightfold Path is as follows:

1. Regarding what is unwholesome

To practice the Eightfold Path with the intention to prevent bad conduct from arising at all in this life and the following existences, is the first kind of right effort.

2. Regarding what is unwholesome

To practice the Eightfold Path with the intention to prevent bad conduct which has not yet arisen for oneself in this life but which is liable to arise in the future, from arising at all until one attains the Nibbāna without remainder of grasping, is the second kind of right effort.

3. Regarding what is wholesome

To make effort in practicing the Eightfold Path in such a way as to attain without fail the higher purities (*visuddhi*) which have not yet been attained in this life, is the third kind of right effort.

4. Regarding what is wholesome

To make effort in such a way as to keep unbroken one's purity of moral conduct—the five precepts and the precepts with livelihood as the eighth (*ājīvaṭṭhamaka-sīla,* for this see below) which one observes in this life until one attains Nibbāna when they become permanent—this is the fourth kind of right effort.

These four are the right efforts which have been explained in this way for easy understanding. They are four in number only with reference to their four functions (namely: avoiding, overcoming, developing, maintaining). But really there is only one factor here—effort or *viriya*—for the reason that when one tries to attain to any of the purities, the effort so exercised covers these four functions automatically.

Here ends the exposition of the four kinds of right effort.

VII. Right Mindfulness

The minds of most beings are never steady but fly about here and there. They have no control over their minds and so cannot fix them steadily on a subject of meditation. As they cannot control their minds they resemble mad or mentally deranged persons and for such people society has no regard. So people who begin to meditate find that their uncontrolled minds resemble those of persons who are deranged. To eliminate the unsteady and flighty mind and to fix it continuously on the meditation subject one has to practice the four applications of mindfulness. They are:

*1. The application of mindfulness to contemplate the body (**kāyānupassanā-satipaṭṭhāna**)*

This means that one's mind is firmly bound to the body-group by the rope of right mindfulness. What is meant here is that the mind is constantly looking at or concentrating upon bodily phenomena, such as breathing in and out and the other exercises listed in the discourse on the application of mindfulness.[43] When such practice has been continued for three or four months, the unsteadiness of the mind disappears and it is possible all the time to concentrate the mind upon the body group. This requires steady practice from day to day which may be from just an hour, or up to six hours daily, upon mindfulness of breathing in and out or one of the other subjects listed in the above discourse. At this point the meditator has control of his mind so that it can be fixed on any meditation subject.

2. *The application of mindfulness to contemplate feeling (**vedanānupassanā-satipaṭṭhāna**)*

This means that one's mind is firmly bound by the rope of right mindfulness to the feeling group (i.e. pleasant feeling, painful feeling, neither painful nor pleasant feeling), which occur all the time in the body varying according to conditions. Repeatedly fixing the mind on these feelings will put an end to restlessness of mind, and when this occurs then one has mental control so that the mind will be concentrated on any subject of meditation.

3. *The application of mindfulness to contemplate mind (**cittānupassanā-satipaṭṭhāna**)*

Here the meaning is that the mindful mind is firmly bound with the mindfulness-rope to the contemplation of the mind when it is associated with greed and

43 See translations in *The Heart of Buddhist Meditation*, Nyanaponika Thera (Kandy, BPS); *The Way of Mindfulness*, Soma Thera (Kandy, BPS); *The Foundations of Mindfulness*, Nyanasatta Thera (BPS Wheel No. 19); *Middle Length Sayings*; Vol. I, Discourse 10, I.B. Horner (PTS London); *The Mahāsatipaṭṭhāna Sutta – The Great Discourse on the Establishing of Awareness*, Vipassana Research Institute (India, VRI).

aversion, which have been present in one's mental continuum from time to time according to conditions. When this is often practiced the restless mind disappears and the mind becomes workable so that it can be fixed on any meditation subject.

4. The application of mindfulness to contemplate dhammas (***dhammānupassanā-satipaṭṭhāna***)[44]

The rope of right mindfulness here binds the mind to the contemplation of such mental objects as sensual desire, ill will, mental and physical sloth, distraction and worry, and uncertainty (i.e. the five hindrances) and other subjects given in the discourse which arise conditionally in one's mind-continuum. When this has been repeated many times restlessness disappears and with this mind-control the mind can be directed to any subject of meditation.

So the applications of mindfulness really mean the meditative work of getting rid of the mad, deranged, hot and burning states of mind that have always formed part of one's mental continuity from successive past lives, by binding the mind with the mindfulness-rope to four of the five groups comprising oneself. Thus body-contemplation is applied to the *body*, feeling-contemplation to the *feelings*, mind-contemplation to *consciousness*, and dhamma-contemplation to *mental formations*. This should be done diligently and regularly in daily prac-

---

44 Here this means subjects which are discovered through close scrutiny of the mind. Such subjects as the five hindrances to meditation, the five groups or aggregates which compose what is called "self," the six internal and external sense spheres (with mind and mind-objects as the sixth), the seven factors of enlightenment, and the Four Noble Truths. See the discourse for details.

tice so that the mind does not stray to external objects but is centered upon the four groups mentioned above.

VIII. Right Concentration

In the world, when one is learning how to read one has to begin with the letters of the alphabet and it is only when these have been mastered that higher education can be acquired. The same principle applies to the process of mental development where mindfulness must be practiced first, for only when it is strong will the mad, deranged mind be got rid of and only then can the higher stages of meditation be practiced with steadfastness.

So when the work of the applications of mindfulness is in order and one is able to concentrate the mind without disturbance for one or two hours or more daily upon one of the exercises in the contemplations of the body, feeling, etc., one should turn to the development of the pure mind (*cittavisuddhi-bhāvanā*), known also as the four levels of collectedness acquired by the practice of calm (*samatha-jhāna-samādhi*). This can be compared to the higher Buddhist studies on the Discourse on Blessings, the passages for paying respect (to the Triple Gem and to one's teachers), the protection discourses, Pāli grammar, and the Manual on the Meaning of Abhidhamma,[45] which are mastered after having learnt the alphabet first.

Among these four levels of collectedness, the first is called the first jhāna and is attained by intense prac-

45 The Pāli in the first edition runs: Maṅgala Sutta, Namakkāra, Paritta, (Grammar and), Abhidhammattha-saṅgaha.

tice of one of the meditation subjects listed below, after having passed through three successive stages of development (*bhāvanā*): the preparatory work on development (*parikamma-bhāvanā*), the access development (*upacāra-bhāvanā*), and the attainment development (*appanā-bhāvanā*). The twenty-five meditation subjects (*kammaṭṭhāna*) for attaining the first jhāna are:

10 kinds of *kasiṇa* devices (4 colors, 4 elements, space, light)
10 kinds of unattractiveness (decaying corpses)
1 exercise on the 32 parts of the body
1 exercise on mindful breathing in and out
3 kinds of divine abidings:
loving kindness (*mettā*)
compassion (*karuṇā*)
joy-with-others (*muditā*).[46]

When a person takes up meditation and makes an effort with the exercise of mindfully breathing in and out, this "preparatory work on development," which is just to get rid of the mad and deranged mind, is included in the first jhāna.

It should be noted that the practice of applying mindfulness to breathing in and out serves both purposes: the establishing of mindfulness and the attainment of the first jhāna. For a full explanation of the four jhānas *The Path of Purification* should be consulted.

Here ends the section on the four kinds of right concentration.

This concludes the full explanation of the Noble Eightfold Path.

---

46 For all these subjects of meditation described in detail see *The Path of Purification* (*Visuddhimagga*), trans. Ñāṇamoli Thera (BPS).

Practicing the Path

The Three Rounds and the Four Kinds of Wandering-On

In the present time, while the Buddhasāsana still exists, if people practice and develop the Noble Eightfold Path they can free themselves from the suffering of the rounds (*vaṭṭa*). I shall explain them to you.

There are three kinds of *suffering* produced by the rounds, and these are:

(1) the round of defilement (*kilesa-vaṭṭa*);
(2) the round of intentional action (*kamma-vaṭṭa*);
(3) the round of resultants (*vipāka-vaṭṭa*).

They are also classified in this way:

(a) the three rounds connected with the wandering-on in states of deprivation;
(b) the three rounds connected with the wandering-on in the good bourns of the sensual realm;
(c) the three rounds connected with the wandering-on in the realms of subtle form;
(d) the three rounds connected with the wandering-on in the realms of formlessness.

(a) In the case of the three rounds connected with the wandering-on in states of deprivation:

(1) the round of defilements refers to personality view and uncertainty;

(2) the round of intentional action refers to the ten evil paths of kamma;
(3) the round of resultants refer to the five resultant kamma-produced groups (*khandha*) of hell-beings, animals, ghosts, and demons.

(b) In the case of the three rounds connected with the wandering-on in the good bourns of the sensual realm:

(1) the round of defilements refers to desire for sensual pleasures, such as pleasant sights, sounds, smells, tastes, and touches;
(2) the round of intentional action refers to the three ways of making merit (good kamma), that is, by giving, moral conduct, and meditation;
(3) the round of resultants refers to the five resultant kamma-produced groups (*khandha*) of human beings and of devas in the six deva-planes.

(c) & (d) In the case of the three rounds connected with the wandering-on in subtle form, or those of formlessness:

(1) the round of defilements refers to attachment to subtle form or formlessness in the realm of subtle form, or the realm of formlessness, respectively;
(2) the round of intentional action refers to wholesome kamma leading to and practiced in the form and formless realms;
(3) the round of resultants refers to the five resultant kamma-produced groups (*khandha*) of the Brahma-gods in the form realm, and to the four resultant mental groups of the Brahma-gods in the formless realm.

So one should understand that there are these three rounds in both form realm and formless realm.

This is the end of the exposition of the three rounds with the four divisions of each of them.

Path-Factors and Rounds

The Eightfold Path may also be divided as it pertains to the experience of stream-winners, once-returners, non-returners, and arahants.

The Eightfold Path, as it is experienced by a person who becomes a stream-winner (at the time when the mind turns away from continuance in the wandering-on towards Nibbāna), completely terminates the three rounds connected with rebirth in the states of deprivation (*apāya*). As regards the rounds connected with wandering-on in the sensual good bourns, it completely terminates all the three rounds that would otherwise arise after seven more existences.[47]

The once-returner's Eightfold Path completely terminates two of the three rounds, the defilements-round and the resultants-round, connected with the realm of sensuality which would otherwise arise in the last five of the seven existences (spoken of above). In other words, the once-returner completely terminates all the three rounds connected with good birth in the sensual realm in two more lives.[48]

The non-returner's Eightfold Path completely terminates the rounds connected with fortunate birth in the sensual realm and goes beyond the two existences of a

---

47 A stream-winner may undergo a maximum of seven more lives, none of them below human level.

48 The once-returner will be reborn once again as a human being or a deva and in that life attain Nibbāna.

once-returner, leaving only the rounds for existence in the form realm and the formless realm.

The path, as it is experienced by a person who attains arahantship, completely terminates the three rounds connected with wandering-on in the form and formless realms. All defilements are forever extinguished.

This concludes the explanation of the inter-relation between path-factors and rounds.

The First, Second, and Third Levels of Views

The three rounds connected with the states of deprivation, among all the four kinds of wandering-on each with its three rounds, are of great urgency for Buddhists today. As Lord Buddha has said, it is a matter of the greatest urgency when one's head is on fire to extinguish it immediately. No delay is possible even for a minute. Well, it is *more* urgent for followers of Buddhism to terminate completely the three rounds connected with the deprived states than for that man to put out the fire on his head. For this reason I have dealt with the Noble Eightfold Path as it is able to terminate those three rounds.[49] How does it do so?

---

49 Venerable Nyanaponika Mahāthera writes: "The Noble Eightfold Path intended here seems to be noble (*ariya*) in the strict sense of the noble path of stream-winner, etc. And when on the latter, *apāya-saṃsāra* is actually cut off because *sīla* (moral conduct) is unbroken and unbreakable. I feel that it is just the absence of *personality view* and *uncertainty* (*sakkāya-diṭṭhi, vicikicchā*) that makes *sīla* finally unbreakable, not just normal restraint. The unwholesome kamma-paths are extreme forms of unwholesomeness, covetousness (*abhijjhā*) which is the greedy thought leading to robbery, or ill will (*byāpāda*) the hateful thought of killing or harming—which are absent in the stream-winner though he has still the milder forms called sensual desire

Among these two defilements (cut off by the stream-winner)—personality view and uncertainty—personality view is the most important. When this view is no more, naturally there is no more uncertainty and the ten unwholesome paths of kamma can no longer be created so that the wandering-on in deprived states is extinguished.

Personality view is just another name for self view (*atta-diṭṭhi*) in which the eye, ear, nose, tongue, body, and mind are regarded as "I" and "mine." This view is held tenaciously by all ordinary people (*puthujjana*). When we say that the sense organs are tenaciously viewed as "I" and "mine," this means that whenever a visible object is seen, people firmly and tenaciously believe "I see it, I see it." The same is true of the other senses and their objects (with mind as the sixth). This is how personality view is established on the foundation of the six internal bases.

Let us take the example of a being who in past lives has made many stupid mistakes so that in his successive lives all these old evil kammas born of personality view are attached to and always accompany his life continuity. Proceeding in such a way, this being will in future existences also make foolish mistakes, thus making new evil kamma arising from personality view. So when

---

(*kāmacchanda*) and aversion (*paṭigha*) among the ten fetters. As he still has the fetters of sensual desire, attachment to subtle form and formlessness (*rūparāga, arūparāga*), rebirth in the good bourns (*sugati*) has not ceased for him. He, being on the path of seeing (*dassana-magga*), has abolished only the *view-root* of self-view (i.e. personality view); its other two roots, craving and conceit, are abolished only on the three noble paths called the path of development (*bhāvanā-magga*). The complete cutting off of personality view is not however a purely intellectual process; it must be based on perfect *sīla* and the *vipassanā* experience."

personality view is extinguished, the results of past evil kamma leading to subhuman birth cannot arise, nor can more evil kamma be made. For this reason there is no longer any possibility of wandering-on in the deprived states; for such a person there are no more rebirths in the hells, the animal world, the ghost realm, and the demons—these are all extinguished. A person like this attains to his first experience of Nibbāna, called Nibbāna-with-the-grasped-at-groups-remaining (*sa-upādisesa nibbāna*), meaning that for him the three rounds connected with the wandering-on in the states of deprivation are utterly extinct. He then becomes a noble one (*ariya*) in the noble supermundane plane, one to be reborn in successively higher planes of existence.[50]

Now we come to consider the three levels of views whereby personality view is established.

The first is called the *latency level* (*anusaya-bhūmi*), that is, the view of personality which always accompanies the life-continuity of a being in the beginningless round of rebirths and resides in the whole person[51] as the seed or potential for the three kinds of kamma, i.e. of body, speech, and mind, before they are made. When objects which can cause the doing of evil deeds come into contact with any of the six doors, such as the eye-door, unwholesome kamma stimulated by that latent

---

50 See the extensive notes on this subject in *The Requisites of Enlightenment*, BPS Pariyatti Edition (BPE) pp. 89-93.

51 Myanaung U Tin writes: "Actually *anusaya* (potentiality) does not reside in any part of the person. It arises only with the necessary conditions. For want of a better word "reside" has been used. Potentiality is there in the whole personality, that is all." The seven latent tendencies or proclivities (*anusaya*) are: sensual desire, aversion, views, uncertainty, conceit, desire for existence, and ignorance.

view is made in the mind. This is the second level called *obsessive level (pariyuṭṭhāna-bhūmi)*, represented among the ten unwholesome paths of kamma by the threefold mental kamma (covetousness, ill-will, and wrong view). Thus the stage of mental kamma has been reached. If no steps are taken for the control of the mind, then unwholesomeness spreads from the obsessive level to the third level called the *transgressive level* (*vītikkama-bhūmi*), the stage where unwholesome verbal or bodily kamma is made. These are, respectively, the fourfold verbal action (false speech, tale-bearing, harsh talk, and useless chatter), and the threefold bodily action (killing living creatures, taking what is not given, wrong conduct in sexual pleasures).

Suppose we take the example of a match. When the matchbox with its nitrous surface is available then the potential for fire lying in the match head can be activated. Flames result and with such a lighted match a heap of rubbish can be set alight. The matchbox's striking surface represents the six sense objects—sights, sounds, smells, tastes, touches, and thoughts—and the potential for fire in the match head may be compared to the latency level. When these objects present themselves to the mind, like the striking of the match, then heat and fire result—the obsessive level. From that small fire a great one can be lighted, burning and scorching other beings with the bodily and verbal kamma of the transgressive level.

This concludes the explanation of the first, second, and third levels of views.

Forming the Path into Three Groups

The Noble Eightfold Path falls naturally into the following groups:

(1) Morality group: right speech, right action, and right livelihood.
(2) Concentration group: right effort, right mindfulness, and right concentration.
(3) Wisdom group: right view and right thought.

If the three constituents of the morality group are considered in detail then they become the set of precepts with livelihood as the eighth, in this way:

> I shall refrain from killing living creatures.
> I shall refrain from taking what is not given.
> I shall refrain from wrong conduct in sexual pleasures and from intoxicants—
> these three comprise *right action*.
>
> I shall refrain from false speech.
> I shall refrain from tale-bearing.
> I shall refrain from harsh talk.
> I shall refrain from useless chatter—
> these four comprise *right speech*.

I undertake *right livelihood*, refraining from dishonesty, violence, and killing.

Permanent precepts, that is, those which are taken to be kept all the time, such as the lay person's Five Precepts, the Ten Precepts observed by hermits and wanderers (perhaps non-Buddhist), and the Ten Precepts practiced by Buddhist novices (*sāmaṇeras*), together with the bhikkhu's 227 precepts contained in the Pātimokkha, are generally contained within the group of precepts with livelihood as the eighth. In the same way, the Eight Precepts are improvements on the Five Precepts and the above group of precepts with livelihood as the eighth.

Right speech, action, and livelihood, which are the constituents of the morality group, are the factors to use for the destruction of the third level of personality view, the transgressive level, when evil unwholesome kamma, fourfold of speech and threefold of bodily action, is committed.

Right effort, mindfulness, and concentration, the factors of the concentration group, are the factors to use for the destruction of the second level of personality view, the obsessive level, when the threefold evil unwholesome kamma of the mind is made.

Right view and right intention, comprising the wisdom group, are the factors to use for the destruction of the first level of personality view, the latency level, which has always existed in the life-continuities of beings in the beginningless round of rebirths.

Here ends the formation of the Eightfold Path into three groups.

How to Establish the Morality Group

To rid oneself of the three unwholesome verbal deeds born of personality view, the three constituents of the morality group must be established in oneself, which is another way of saying that the set of precepts with livelihood as eighth should be accepted and practiced.

One cannot guard against the three unwholesome mental deeds born of personality view in this way, so when one no longer wishes to make them, the three factors of the concentration group in the Noble Eightfold

Path should be practiced and established. Such firmness of mind only results when exercises such as mindfulness of in-and-out breathing, or the meditation on the unattractiveness of such things as bones, or the meditations on colors, elements, etc., called *kasiṇas*, are practiced *for at least one hour a day*.

The method whereby one may rid oneself of the transgressive level of personality view is by establishing oneself in purification of virtue as represented by the set of precepts with livelihood as the eighth, as mentioned above. One may either first recite the precepts, as given below, and then practice them, or just decide to observe them so that from this day forth, throughout one's life, one does not kill living creatures, etc. It is not necessary to request these precepts from a bhikkhu; one has only to practice them accordingly. One may then either recite or determine, as follows:

(1) From today throughout my life, I shall refrain from killing any living creatures.
(2) From today throughout my life, I shall refrain from taking what is not given.
(3) From today throughout my life, I shall refrain from wrong conduct in sexual pleasures and from intoxicants.
(4) From today throughout my life, I shall refrain from false speech.
(5) From today throughout my life, I shall refrain from setting one person against another.
(6) From today throughout my life, I shall refrain from harsh and abusive words regarding any person's status in society and beliefs.
(7) From today throughout my life, I shall refrain from speaking in ways not conducive to the welfare of beings in this present life, or of those in the

wandering-on, or of those in the supermundane plane.[52]

(8) From today throughout my life, I shall refrain from wrong livelihood.

When this set of precepts has been taken, it remains in force until it is broken. Then only the precept which has been broken should be undertaken once again, though of course there is no harm in taking again those precepts which have not been broken. This is really unnecessary, but if an unbroken precept is taken again it will be strengthened in this way.

It is better, therefore, to undertake these precepts everyday. But these precepts are permanent, that is, they apply every day, like the Five Precepts. They are not like the Eight Precepts observed only on the Uposatha days. Bhikkhus who have 227 precepts and sāmaṇeras who observe ten precepts, as well as hermits and wanderers, need not take these precepts.

Now the constituent factors which are required for the breaking of the first seven of these precepts should be examined.

The five conditions for killing living creatures

(1) The being must be alive.
(2) There must be the knowledge that it is a living being.
(3) There must be an intention to cause its death.
(4) Action must be taken to cause its death.
(5) Death must result from such action.

If all these five conditions are fulfilled then the first precept has been broken and should be taken again.

---

52 Such as arahants living now.

The five conditions for taking what is not given

(1) The property must be the possession of another person.
(2) It must be known to oneself that it is the possession of another person.
(3) There must be an intention to steal.
(4) Action must be taken to steal.
(5) By that action the property must be taken.

If all these five conditions are fulfilled then the second precept has been broken and should be taken again.

The four conditions for wrong conduct in sexual pleasures

(1) There must be a man or a woman with whom it is improper to have sexual intercourse.[53]
(2) There must be intention to have sexual intercourse with such a person.
(3) Action must be taken to have such intercourse.
(4) There must be enjoyment from the contact of the sexual organs.

If all these four conditions are fulfilled then the third precept has been broken and should be taken again.

The four conditions for false speech

(1) The statement must be untrue.
(2) There must be an intention to deceive.
(3) There must be an effort made as a result of this intention.

---

53 Bhikkhus, bhikkhunīs, and other religious observing the holy life, or persons protected by marriage or by parents.

(4) The other person must know the meaning of what has been said.

If all these four conditions are fulfilled then the fourth precept has been broken and should be taken again.

The four conditions for tale-bearing

(1) There must be persons to be disunited.
(2) There must be the intention to disunite these persons.
(3) There must be an effort made as a result of this intention.
(4) The other person(s) must know the meaning of what has been said.

If all these four conditions are fulfilled then the fifth precept has been broken and should be taken again.

The three conditions for harsh talk

(1) There must be a person to be abused.
(2) There must be anger.
(3) Harsh language must be directed towards that person.

If all these three conditions are fulfilled then the sixth precept has been broken and should be taken again.

The two conditions for useless chatter

(1) There must be intention to say things which bring forth no wholesome benefits.
(2) Such things must be said.

If these conditions are fulfilled then the seventh precept has been broken and should be taken again.

As regards "things which bring forth no wholesome benefits," this means plays and novels which do not lead to the growth of good qualities. Nowadays we have numerous plays and novels which satisfy all the conditions of useless chatter.

Fulfilment of the conditions given above for the first three precepts and for harsh speech, the sixth one, are sufficient not only to break these but also to make kamma which will be a "path of kamma" leading to rebirth in the states of deprivation. But in the case of the precepts dealing with false speech, tale-bearing, and useless chatter, the following have to be added if these actions are to be paths of kamma:

(1) In the case of false speech, another person suffers loss or damage.
(2) In the case of tale-bearing, disunion must be brought about.
(3) And in the case of useless chatter, others must think that the plays and novels are true accounts.

These are the conditions relating to the seven kinds of wrong-doing which should be known by those who daily keep the precepts with livelihood as the eighth.

And this concluses the brief explanation of the way to establish in oneself the three constituents of the path's morality group.

How to Establish the Concentration Group

As we have explained already, the good practice of the three constituents of the morality group leads to the establishment in the purity of moral conduct, while wrong livelihood and the seven kinds of bad conduct, three with the body and four with speech—which are all born of personality view—are completely cut off.

Then, in order destroy the second level of wrong view supported by the three mental evil kammas, the factors of the concentration group in the Eightfold Path—right effort, right mindfulness, and right concentration—must be established in oneself.

By this is meant practice of one of the forty subjects of meditation. Here the way of practice for "mindfulness of breathing in and out" will be described briefly. If Buddhist householders have no time during the day to do this practice, they should do it everyday without fail in the early morning after rising, say for an hour, and in the evening too, for one or two hours before going to bed.

The method to follow in this practice is as follows. According to the Buddha-word: "*Mindfully he breathes in, mindfully he breathes out.*" So during the whole period during which one has determined to sit, the mind is concentrated just on the breathing and is not allowed to stray here and there. To accomplish this one needs bodily effort and mental effort. Here, bodily effort means the effort made to practice for a fixed period each day, never letting a day go by without practice. Mental effort is the extreme care that one takes when breathing in and out that the mind may not stray elsewhere, as well as the intense application of the mind to the meditation subject so that sleepiness and sloth do not creep in.

As the breath touches the nostrils during exhalation one should be mindful just of the breathing out. Similarly, when inhaling be mindful just of the touch of air passing in. The mind should be fixed continuously upon the region of the nostrils. So right effort here means these two kinds of effort, bodily and mental, as mentioned above.

When one applies the mind in this way for a fortnight, a month, or even two months, one's mindfulness becomes fixed upon breathing in and out. Such mindfulness is indeed called right mindfulness.

And once the three factors of the morality group in this path have been established, mental restlessness decreases day by day.

It is apparent to everyone who begins meditation practice that they have no control over the mind as far as meditation subjects are concerned. Now in this world madmen who have no control over their minds are useless in worldly affairs. In like manner it can be said of people thought sane by this world that, as regards the practice of meditation, they are really mad, for they have no control over the meditation subject. Such people are useless when judged by the standard needed for successful meditation practice. When viewed in this way, we can see the necessity for the establishment of the three factors of the concentration group so that restlessness of mind is cured.[54]

Even though the two aspects of concentration called access concentration and attainment concentration (*upacāra*-and *appanā-samādhi*) have not yet been attained, if the mind can be fixed on the meditation subject for a period of an hour or two every day then it will become easy to concentrate the mind whenever one wishes and on whatever meditation subject one takes up.

For a person who has attained purity of mind after being successful in establishing the three factors of the concentration group in the Noble Eightfold Path, the three unwholesome mental kammas of covetousness,

---

54 For more detailed information about right concentration see *The Requisites of Enlightenment* and *Ānāpānadīpanī* .

ill-will, and wrong view born of personality view become extinct. And the second level (obsessive) of views represented by the above three mental kammas is also extinguished. Again, the mental restlessness caused by the five hindrances also disappears.

This concludes the explanation of how to establish the three factors of the concentration group of the Eightfold Path.

From the time when the factors of the morality group become established in a person, so long as he does not violate them he is said to be complete in the purity of moral conduct. On the very day when the precepts are perfectly established, the concentration group—right effort, right mindfulness, and right concentration—should be practiced. Now people who are reasonably diligent should not take more than five or ten days to rid themselves of mental restlessness. Having done so and attained a steadfast concentration of mind on breathing in and out, the three factors of the concentration group are established. From that day one is said to have established oneself in purity of mind. One should then go on to establish the wisdom group of the Eightfold Path in oneself.

How to Establish the Wisdom Group

Right View

Whoever has been successful in establishing purity of moral conduct and purity of mind should then try to establish the wisdom group of right view and right intention so as to destroy the latency level of personality view. To have established these two path factors means the establishment in due order of the five purities of wisdom, which are: purity of view, purity of overcoming doubt, purity by knowledge and vision of what is and what is not the path, purity by knowledge and vision of the practice-path, purity by supermundane knowledge and vision.

To bring this about, we should consider the four great primaries which are, literally, earth, water, fire, and air. Let us look at them in relation to the body. Hardness and softness make up the earth (extension) element; cohesion and liquidity comprise the water element; heat and cold compose the fire (kinetic energy) element; while support and motion are the characteristics of the air element. In the case of the head there are only these four elements present and the same applies to the rest of the body—legs, arms, head-hair, body-hair, nails, teeth, skin, flesh, sinews, bones, marrow, kidneys, heart, lymph, fat, lungs, intestines, stomach, excrement, and brains. All are just collections of the four elements.

If we look at them we can see:

(1) hardness is the strong form of *earth*, softness the weak;
(2) cohesion is the weak form of *water*, liquidity the strong;
(3) heat is the strong form of *fire*, cold the weak;
(4) stillness is the weak form of *air*, motion the strong.

Now to consider these in pairs.

Let us take the example of sealing wax, in which the various changes can be observed. In its usual state, hardness, the strong form of earth, is conspicuous. But when it comes into contact with fire, the hard earth element disappears and soft earth is manifest. But when the fire is removed then the softness naturally disappears and hardness reappears.

In the case of cohesion or liquidity, in its usual state sealing wax shows a weak form of water so that cohesion is present. But with contact of fire the cohesive water element disappears and liquid water is manifest. Again, if the fire is taken away then liquidity disappears while cohesiveness becomes manifest again.

As regards heat and cold, in its usual state sealing wax has weak fire element while coldness is conspicuous. When there is contact with fire the cold fire element vanishes and is replaced by hot fire, but by its removal the process is naturally reversed.

Lastly, considering stillness and motion, sealing wax in its usual state shows a weak form of air, that is, stillness. But when it is heated a strong form of the air element is manifest: motion. With the removal of the fire, however, the strong form naturally disappears and the weak form returns.

This example has been given so that people are able to understand the meaning of arising and passing away (*udayabbaya*) in insight or vipassanā. The word '*udaya*' means arising, increase, or appearance, while '*vaya*' has the meaning of passing away, decrease, or disappearance. '*Udayabbaya*' is the compound of the two words. These elements are evident in the sealing wax. Now we shall turn to their practical application.

Head, body, legs, and hands can all be analyzed in the same way as the sealing wax so that the elements become clear. For instance, heat and cold, the two aspects of the fire element, arise and pass away alternately. Heat increases little by little in the body from sunrise until two in the afternoon, after which the body begins to cool, meaning that heat decreases and cold increases. This is everyone's experience. We easily understand that the same is true of other bodily processes as well.

The increase in the body heat in the head and so forth is like the sealing wax coming into contact with the fire, while as coolness increases in the body it resembles the sealing wax from which the fire has been removed. This increase and decrease of the fire element in the body is the arising and passing away spoken of above.

So too with the other three elements; their pairs of modes also arise and pass away like the fire element. Earth element with its modes of softness and hardness, water element seen as liquidity and cohesion, and air element in its forms of motion and stillness—they increase or decrease in the same way.

These four elements in the body resemble the innumerable tiny bubbles quickly appearing and disappearing on the surface of a big pot of boiling water. The whole body, in fact, resembles a lump of foam. Vapor appears in each small bubble and it bursts to disappear as all the rest disappear.

It is the same with seeing, hearing, smell, taste, touch, and knowing. All these mental phenomena depend on the four elements and vanish when the elements vanish. So the six consciousnesses—of eye, ear, nose, tongue, body, and mind—together with the four elements are impermanent, transitory, and unstable. They are all *anicca* (impermanent) and therefore *dukkha* (unsatisfactory), too, since they are associated with unceasing arising and passing away; and such transient and unsatisfactory phenomena are therefore also *anattā* (not self or not soul) because they are without essence or substance.

Taking the head as an example, let us see how personality view arises on the basis of the four elements and how it should really be seen with right view. People who cannot discriminate the four elements in the head do not understand that the head's solidity is only the earth element. They understand that it is head, and so on; they perceive a "head," they conceive "my head," they view it as "my permanent head," taking it as an unchanging entity.

Understanding that "it is head" is a delusion of mind (*citta*).

Perceiving "a head" is delusion of perception (*saññā*).

Conceiving "my head" is delusion of conceit (*māna*).

Holding a view of it as "my permanent head" is a delusion of view (*diṭṭhi*).[55]

Understanding, perceiving, conceiving, and holding a view of the head, instead of directly seeing it as four elements, is viewing it as permanent and as *attā* or self. Thus to consider the four elements as the head is a fallacy based on taking what is impermanent as permanent, and what is not self as self.

These four elements, which naturally arise and pass away extremely rapidly, are truly impermanent and not self, thus illustrating the Buddha's words:

---

55 The first, second, and third items are the three perversions or distortions (*vipallāsa*), on which see *The Manual of Insight* BPS Pariyatti Edition (BPE).

"*Khayaṭṭhena aniccaṃ asārakaṭṭhena anattā*," meaning, "Because it is destroyed it is impermanent, because it is essenceless it is not self." The head of a man does not normally break up during his life, nor does it disintegrate when he dies; it remains looking much the same until the body reaches the burning ground. For these reasons it is regarded as permanent and taken to be self. When the four elements are not penetrated with insight, then the misconception "head" arises, taking what is changing as unchanging and what is not self as self.

Understanding, perceiving, conceiving, and viewing hair, teeth, skin, flesh, muscles, bones, brain, as the composite parts of the head, rather than penetrating them with insight as the four elements alone, is taking what is impermanent as permanent, not self as self. It is just personality view to see the elements, such as hardness, as head, hair, and so on. Such a view displays ignorance (*avijjā*).

Right view (acquired by insight) sees that hardness is the earth element, not a part of "my body" such as bones. In the same way cohesion is the water element, heat and cold the fire element, and stillness and motion the air element. They are not to be seen as my hair, my teeth, my flesh, my brain. In the ultimate analysis (made in deep meditation, not by intellectual effort), there is no such thing as the head or its parts. Such penetration is called right view. It is not necessary to emphasize that what has been said here about the head—the personality view which depends on wrong view, and the right view which arises when the view of a "person" is abandoned—applies to all the other parts of the body, too.

Right Thought

To consider ways and means for understanding these four elements is right thought. While right view may be compared to an arrow, right thought is the strength in the hand that aims the arrow at the target. In brief this is how right view and right thought, the two factors of the wisdom group in the Noble Eightfold Path, should be established in oneself. For detailed explanations, see the *Vijjāmagga-dīpanī* and the *Bhāvanā-dīpanī* written by me.

The Need for Effort

These two factors of the wisdom group are established by continual contemplation and deep meditation upon arising and passing away (*udayabbaya*). This means the incessant arisings and passings of the four elements in their combinations throughout the body in all its parts, beginning with head hair, and so forth. It applies also to the six kinds of sense consciousness—of the eye, ear, nose, tongue, body, and mind—where arising and passing continue without any break. All this can be compared to the small bubbles in a pot of boiling water. Now when this insight has been established in oneself and when some insight has thereby been gained into the characteristics of impermanence and not self, one must make effort to continue in the direction of complete penetration throughout one's life, so that stage by stage the paths and fruits are won.

To take an example of how this may be done: farmers in the course of their cultivation should practice contemplation on the arising and the passing of the psychophysical elements in all parts of the body.

So by repeated and persistent practice of this meditation, there is born the (insight) knowledge of right view regarding the arising and passing of all physical and psychological phenomena. Such knowledge permeates the whole body, and at this time the first level of personality view regarding the body as "mine" disappears. In this way the latency level view of the body as a person, which has accompanied one's life-continuity throughout the beginningless round of rebirths, is extinguished without remainder. The whole body is then transformed into the sphere of right view. Potential for making the ten unwholesome kammas is totally destroyed while the ten wholesome ways of making kamma are firmly established. The round of rebirth in the states of deprivation is destroyed for such a person and there remain for him only rebirths in the good bourns, such as among human beings, devas and Brahmās. The person has attained the level of a noble one, a stream-winner.[56]

So this brings to a close the exposition of personality view as illustrated by the head and concludes as well the full explanation of the practice of the Noble Eightfold Path with its three factors of the morality group, three in the concentration group, and two in the wisdom group.

How to Establish the Noble Eightfold Path

Complete and careful observance of the set of precepts with livelihood as the eighth is the practice of the morality group comprising right speech, right action, and right livelihood. The practice of the mindful breathing in and out is the concentration group of right effort, right, mindfulness, and right concentration put into action. Contemplation of arising and passing of the

---

56 The original has a "*bon-sin-san* noble one." See *The Requisites of Enlightenment*, p.41.

four elements as illustrated by the head, and of the six sense consciousnesses, makes up the wisdom group comprising right view and right thought.

According to the method followed by the dry-visioned person (*sukkha-vipassaka puggala*), the way of calm (*samatha*) through such exercises as mindfully breathing in and out is not practiced separately. Such a person, having established in himself the three factors of the morality group in the Eightfold Path, then undertakes the practice of the wisdom group. In this practice the three constituents of the concentration group accompany the two wisdom factors and are together known as the path with five factors (*pañcaṅgika-magga*). These five, in such practice, form one group and with the three remaining factors, the morality group, make up the Noble Eightfold Path. But insight-only as practiced by these dry-visioned people can succeed only if one has great penetrative wisdom and makes strenuous effort.[57] Mental restlessness will then disappear as it does with the practice of calm.

After the knowledge of right view has become clear (through meditation) in respect of the whole body, whether such direct knowledge is attained in this life or the next, then whenever one contemplates within, there are no such entities as a person, individual, woman, man, oneself, another person, head, leg, or hair. When such knowledge arises, the personality view which takes hardness and so on to be the head (etc.) disappears

---

57 This warning is needed! It is possible to find teachers who stress that *vipassanā* (insight) only is required and that calm is not necessary. Their pupils, not possessing either great wisdom or strenuous effort, arrive only at weak and easily lost "insight," if they attain anything at all. Such one-sided views produce no good results.

forever. Whenever this contemplation is done, there arises the right view of the truth that "head" does not exist apart from a collection of elements. This principle applies to the other parts of the body.

When right view and right thought, the wisdom factors of the path, have been established in one's personality, then the three rounds connected with wandering-on in the states of deprivation disappear forever. Whoever experiences this is from that moment on completely freed for all time from the suffering arising from these rounds, that is, from the pain and misery of being born in the four lower worlds. He or she has reached and is established in the first experience of Nibbāna with the grasped-at groups remaining and is a stream-winner.[58]

However, as such a person has yet to acquire the knowledge associated with the mark of unsatisfactoriness (*dukkha-lakkhaṇa*)[59] there still remain in him craving (*taṇhā*) and conceit (*māna*) which cause him to delight in the pleasures of men, devas, and Brahmās. So he continues to enjoy these three kinds of pleasures while being reborn in successively higher planes.[60]

Here ends the brief explanation of the way to establish the Eightfold Path in oneself. It is also the conclusion of *The Manual of the Path-Factors* (*Maggaṅga-dīpanī*).

—§§§—

---

58 See the extensive note in *The Requisites of Enlightenment*, pp.41–42.

59 See note 49.

60 See *The Requisites of Enlightenment*, pp.41–42 note.

A Life Sketch of the Venerable Ledi Sayādaw

The author of this manual, the Venerable Ledi Sayādaw of Burma, was one of the outstanding Buddhist scholars and writers of this age. His numerous writings show not only his vast store of learning, of which he had a ready command, but also a deep penetration of the respective subjects derived from his meditative experience. During a long period of his later life he used to spend six months of the year teaching, preaching, and writing, and the other six months meditating.

He was born in 1846 at a village in the Shwebo District of Burma. Early in life he was ordained a novice (*sāmaṇera*) and at the age of twenty he received the higher ordination with the name Bhikkhu Ñāṇa. He received his monastic education under various teachers and later studied Buddhist literature under the Venerable San-kyaung Sayādaw in one of the large monastic colleges at Mandalay. He was a very bright student. His first book, *Pāramī Dīpanī* (*Manual of the Perfections*) was published fourteen years after his higher ordination while he was still at San-kyaung Monastery. It was based on twenty questions set by his teacher, which he alone among the numerous pupils had been able to answer fully and satisfactorily.

During the reign of King Theebaw he became a Pali lecturer at Mahā Jotikārāma Monastery in Mandalay. One year after the capture of King Theebaw, in 1887, he moved to a place to the north of Monywa town where he established a monastery under the name of Ledi-tawya Monastery, from which he derived the name Ledi Sayadaw under which he became widely known. In later years, he regularly toured many parts of Burma, teaching and preaching, and establishing Abhidhamma classes and meditation centres. He composed Abhidhamma rhymes (*abhidhamma-saṅkhitta*) and taught them to his Abhidhamma classes. Some of the Ledi meditation centres still exist and are still famous in the country.

He was awarded the title Agga-Mahāpaṇḍita by the Government of India in 1911. Later the University of Rangoon conferred on him the title D. Litt. (*honoris causa*). In later years he lived at Pyinma where he died in 1923, aged 77.

The Venerable Ledi Sayadaw wrote many essays, letters, poems and manuals, in Burmese and in Pali, and also some sub-commentaries (*ṭīkā*). A list of his writings has been published in the Buddhist quarterly, "Light of the Dhamma" (Vol. VIII, No. 1),[61] together with a biography on which this brief life sketch is based. Most of his expositions are called *dīpanī* ("manuals" or lit. "illuminators"), and became very popular in Burma. Some of these are short treatises; others are larger works, as for instance the *Paramattha Dīpanī, The Manual of Ultimate Truth,* written in 1897, which is a commentary on the *Abhidhammattha Saṅgaha*, a compendium of the Abhidhamma Philosophy.

Several of these manuals seven have been rendered into English and published or reprinted in the magazine "Light of the Dhamma": (1) *Vipassanā Dīpanī—Manual of Insight,* (2) *Paṭṭhānuddesa Dīpanī—Manual of the Philosophy of Relations,* (3) *Niyāma Dīpanī—Manual of Cosmic Order,* (4) *Sammā-diṭṭhi Dīpanī—Manual of Right*

---

61 Published by the Union of Burma Buddha Sāsana Council, Kaba Aye P.O., Rangoon, Burma. An extensive list is also given in the B.P.S. translation of the *Vijjāmagga Dīpanī.*

Understanding, (5) *Catusacca Dīpanī— Manual of the Four Truths*, (6) *Bodhipakkhiya Dīpanī—Manual of the Requisites of Enlightenment*, (7) *Maggaṅga Dīpanī—Manual of the Constituents of the Noble Path.*

The "Light of the Dhamma" has ceased publication, however, the manuals have been reprinted in a single volume under the title *Manuals of Buddhism* published by the aforementioned Council in Rangoon and by the Vipassanā Research Institute in Igatpuri, India.

The BPS has published a few other translations. A revised edition of the *Manual of the Requisites of Enlightenment* has appeared in the Wheel Series as Wheel no. 171/174 (now BP 412), likewise, the *Paṭṭhānuddesa Dīpanī* as Wh. 331/333 titled *Buddhist Philosophy of Relations*, the *Maggaṅga Dīpanī* as Wh. 245/ 247 titled *Noble Eightfold Path and its Factors Explained*, the *Uttamapurisa Dīpanī* as BP 420 titled *Manual of the Excellent Man*, the *Ānāpāna Dīpanī* as Wh. 431/432 titled *A Manual of Mindfulness of Breathing*, and the *Manual of Light (Alinkyan)* and the *Manual of the Path of Higher Knowledge (Vijjāmagga Dīpanī)* as BP 620.

A few more translations of Ledi Sayadaw manuals on vegetarianism, abstinence from liquor, and monks' etiquette can be found on http://www.aimwell.org.

—§§§—